# Cyber Verse

## The Tech Trap

*Vere John Carneiro*

Chennai • Bangalore

CLEVER FOX PUBLISHING
Chennai, India

Published by CLEVER FOX PUBLISHING 2025
Copyright © Vere John Carneiro 2025

All Rights Reserved.
ISBN: 978-93-56489-65-3

This book has been published with all reasonable efforts taken to make the material error-free after the consent of the author. No part of this book shall be used, reproduced in any manner whatsoever without written permission from the author, except in the case of brief quotations embodied in critical articles and reviews.

The Author of this book is solely responsible and liable for its content including but not limited to the views, representations, descriptions, statements, information, opinions and references ["Content"]. The Content of this book shall not constitute or be construed or deemed to reflect the opinion or expression of the Publisher or Editor. Neither the Publisher nor Editor endorse or approve the Content of this book or guarantee the reliability, accuracy or completeness of the Content published herein and do not make any representations or warranties of any kind, express or implied, including but not limited to the implied warranties of merchantability, fitness for a particular purpose. The Publisher and Editor shall not be liable whatsoever for any errors, omissions, whether such errors or omissions result from negligence, accident, or any other cause or claims for loss or damages of any kind, including without limitation, indirect or consequential loss or damage arising out of use, inability to use, or about the reliability, accuracy or sufficiency of the information contained in this book.

# Contents

1. Tweeting Within .................................................. 1
2. Virtual Consciousness ......................................... 3
3. Identity Woes ....................................................... 5
4. Deprogrammed .................................................... 7
5. Digital Dismay ..................................................... 9
6. Data Quagmire .................................................. 11
7. e Contradictions ............................................... 13
8. Hacker's Delight ................................................ 15
9. Money in the Cloud .......................................... 17
10. Robogenesis ....................................................... 19
11. The Machine or Me? ......................................... 21
12. effete Systems ................................................... 23
13. Tech Sanity ........................................................ 25
14. Bittersweet Tweets ............................................ 27
15. Net Love ............................................................ 29
16. d-Vice ................................................................ 31

# Contents

**17.** Stepping out of Reality? ................................................. 33

**18.** Troll Trap ....................................................................... 35

**19.** Gaming Obsession ....................................................... 37

**20.** e-Reality ........................................................................ 39

**21.** e-Truth .......................................................................... 41

**22.** Tech Hell ....................................................................... 43

**23.** i-Pest ............................................................................. 45

**24.** Cyber Bullying ............................................................. 47

**25.** Fake the News! ............................................................. 49

**26.** The Tech Process Stressed Out! ................................... 51

**27.** The Cyber Muddle ....................................................... 53

**28.** The Internet Imbroglio ................................................ 55

**29.** Quantum Quagmire ..................................................... 57

**30.** Intellectual Techtortion ............................................... 59

**31.** Digital Disruption ........................................................ 61

**32.** The Open Screen .......................................................... 63

**33.** Memory Logged Out .................................................... 65

**34.** The Mobile Stalker ....................................................... 67

**35.** Tackling Technositisitis ................................................ 69

**36.** Technonomics .............................................................. 71

**37.** Technojargon Crap! ..................................................... 73

# Contents

**38.** Devilware trap! ........................................................... 75
**39.** Faceless Facial Recognition! ........................................ 77
**40.** The Cyber Attention Syndrome ................................... 79
**41.** Data in your Face! ....................................................... 81
**42.** Cyber Waste – The Great Problem! .............................. 83
**43.** The Blog Imbroglio! ..................................................... 85
**44.** The Web of Destruction! .............................................. 87
**45.** Digital Desolation ........................................................ 89
**46.** Tech Code on the run! .................................................. 91
**47.** The Programming Syndrome ....................................... 93
**48.** The Babel of Tech ........................................................ 95
**49.** Programming the Intellect ........................................... 97
**50.** Where's my Data? ........................................................ 99
**51.** The Social Network Morass! ...................................... 101
**52.** Gaslighting the truth! ................................................. 103
**53.** I'm not a #Hashtag! .................................................... 105
**54.** Poor me, I am an Online Addict! ............................... 107
**55.** Information Overload! ............................................... 109
**56.** Life's Online Gaming Obsession! ............................... 111
**57.** Cyber Trading in the Cyberdump! ............................. 113
**58.** Cyber Intruders! ......................................................... 115

## Contents

**59.** The Information Enigma .......... 117
**60.** The Data Processing Cookbook .......... 119
**61.** The Social Media Addiction! .......... 121
**62.** Virtual Communities stuck in Reality! .......... 123
**63.** Virtual Avatars! .......... 125
**64.** Virtual Worlds! .......... 127
**65.** The Mind Tech Wrangle! .......... 129
**66.** The Digital Divide! .......... 131
**67.** Digital Inclusion or Delusion? .......... 133
**68.** Muddled Algorithms! .......... 135
**69.** Natural Language Processed! .......... 137
**70.** The Devil's in the Defaults! .......... 139
**71.** Trapped in the Web! .......... 141
**72.** Chatbots or Chatterbots .......... 143
**73.** Data commands all! .......... 145
**74.** Tech Dis-Connectivity! .......... 147
**75.** My intimate exclusive Mobile companion! .......... 149
**76.** 'Artificial' Intelligence! .......... 151
**77.** Discriminative Artificial Intelligence! .......... 153
**78.** Generative or Degenerative Artificial Intelligence! .......... 155
**79.** Subjective Intelligence! .......... 157

80. Ambient Intelligence .................................................. 159
81. Rogue Intelligence! .................................................. 161
82. Deep Learning .......................................................... 163
83. The Metaverse Mix up! ............................................ 165
84. Is it Real or is it Virtual? ........................................ 167
85. Tech Addiction! ....................................................... 169
86. Digital Detox ........................................................... 171
87. Apps Galore! ........................................................... 173
88. E- Learning -the Search Engine or the Chatbot? ......... 175
89. e-frauds Galore! ..................................................... 177
90. Where is My Data! .................................................. 179
91. Intelligence and beyond! ......................................... 181
92. End to End Encryption -Really! ............................... 183
93. Human Bits and Bytes! ............................................ 185
94. Digital Insecurity! ................................................... 187
95. 'Artificial Intelligence' the Copycat! ......................... 189
96. Chatbot e-Jurisprudence! ........................................ 191
97. Artificial Intelligence wars! ..................................... 193
98. Machine Vs Human Creativity ................................ 195
99. Print me out in 3D, please! ..................................... 197
100. Nano Robos in my Brain! ........................................ 199

# The Tech Trap

We live in an age where technology is everywhere, from the devices in our hands to the systems that run our cities, our environments and our lives. Technology offers incredible benefits: faster communication, greater efficiency, connectivity, unparalleled convenience, fuelling us with unlimited knowledge making life much easier to live through.

Yet, there's a hidden downside!

The "Tech Trap" refers to the situation where individuals, businesses, or societies become overly reliant on technology, leading to unintended negative consequences.

While technology brings many advantages — it can also create dependencies that diminish critical thinking, creativity, and human skills. Over-automation, data security vulnerabilities, and loss of personal privacy are examples of how the tech trap manifests. We're becoming too reliant. We're losing control. Automation is taking over, data breaches are more frequent, and privacy is slipping away. We may find ourselves trapped in a cycle of constant upgrades, social media pressures, or algorithmic control, losing autonomy over our choices and interactions. Additionally, as technology evolves rapidly, keeping pace can lead to economic disparities, where those without access or skills are left behind. Balancing technology's benefits with mindful use is key to avoiding the "Tech Trap" which the author has brought out in this unique and original literary and artistic presentation, posing a question to all,

"Are you in control, or are you trapped?"

# THE TECH TRAP

*Cryptic Space*

# 1

# TWEETING WITHIN

I question myself,
Tweeting my mind,
Seeking a response,
In cryptic space,
What overwhelms me now,
A deluge of data,
The answers so diverse,
Not a solution to assure,
I struggle within myself,
My life set to a screen,
Searching for enlightenment,
Images float by,
While I wait in anticipation,
My ego tweets incessantly,
Leaving me in this virtual void,
I would rather be free,
My tweets got 'X'ed!

*The muddled uniqueness of my being!*

# 2

# VIRTUAL CONSCIOUSNESS

Am I free?
To explore the depths of my consciousness,
To wander through my imagination,
To step out of reality,
To let me be to myself,
To be what I am to be,
Stepping into virtual space,
So undetermined,
As I set out to wander,
Far beyond the imagination,
What lies in me,
Is in me alone,
I have come alive to myself,
To live within and without myself,
To create my own reality,
Living in a virtual world,
Escaping into nothingness,
The muddled uniqueness of my virtual being!

*Lost in oblivion!*

# 3

# IDENTITY WOES

Who am I?
A number for reckoning,
Trapped in a password,
Somewhere in cryptic space,
A stolen identity,
Lost in oblivion,
Used and misused,
A dot on a screen,
Moved and manipulated,
By the cursor of Life,
One in the absolute,
Stepping in to step out,
Come and gone forever,
A unique character,
From zero to one,
Returning from one to zero,
A blob of matter,
Spliced in time and space,
Wiped out by the intellect!

*Digital Limbo*

# 4

# DEPROGRAMMED

Where am I?
Trapped in a logical existence,
Floundering in digitised space,
Programmed to anticipate,
Endless rational outcomes,
Information flows through,
Formatted for prompt delivery,
Data compressed for posterity,
On a neuron floating in infinity,
Wired for spontaneous recall,
Routed through the system,
On a quest beyond knowledge,
Seeking optimisation from within,
Wading through a virtual world,
Enmeshed in a digital limbo,
Struggling to free the grid,
Opening up Life's menu for display,
The Mind is set free,
Deprogramed to enjoy Life to the fullest!

*Where am I?*

# 5

# DIGITAL DISMAY

Here I am,
Stepping out of hard reality,
Into the vast digital arena,
With free access redefined,
Authenticated offline,
To float free in the cloud,
Till the deluge of data,
Crumbles understanding,
Flowing through the pathways
To clog all communication,
Garbled information flows through,
Churned for immediate processing,
Laid out on a Template,
With knowledge now laid bare,
Nothing remains to back-up,
Emotions follow through,
Exposed then censored,
Crushed feelings,
Where am I?

The Digital Quagmire

# 6

# DATA QUAGMIRE

Here we are,
Servers inundated,
Thrash flows from the bins,
Clogging all processors,
Hackers dribble through,
Searching for a paradigm,
To set fortunes free,
Smudge is analysed,
Filtered through the web,
Making dirt as good as new,
Flowing across the network,
All lies turn to truth,
Facts construed to please,
News made up for gratification,
Information flows out,
Unconstrained and unrestrained,
Flowing in and flowing out,
Through the internet of disconnect,
Into a Digital Quagmire!

*Firewalls ablaze!*

# 7

# E CONTRADICTIONS

Secure systems so isolated,
Access denied to all!
Encrypted code so uninterpretable,
Generating muddled output!
Isolated servers well-spaced out,
Now lost in the cloud!
Optimised performance well attained,
Only to be gapped in analysis!
Input so well secured,
But the keyboard is logged out!
Systems spyware proof and well secured,
But malware intrudes!
Events are managed,
Yet nothing is detected!
Confidential mails,
Phished through!
Remote monitoring,
Lost in oblivion!
All Firewalls are now ablaze!

*Hacker's Delight!*

# 8

# HACKER'S DELIGHT

Skim the net,
Phish the system,
Hijack the router,
Log on to the inputs,
Pick up the keys,
Bypass the passwords,
Scam the metrics,
Covertly break through,
Crypto jack the logs,
Spread out the resources,
Isolate the users,
Decrypt the data,
Reroute the processor,
Block the access,
Garner all privileges,
Muddle the utilities,
Erase the memory,
Challenge validity,
Stealthily log out!

₹ Bits CHF
Rupee        Swiss Franc
     Pound
Bits  £    €    Bits
          Bits EURO  Bits
Bits $
   Dollar YEN    R
        Bits ¥   Rand
Bits              Bits
     Renminbi
        ¥
Bits        ☺
        ₽   Riyal
Bits  Ruble
      Bits   Bits

*Money in the i cloud!*

# 9

# MONEY IN THE CLOUD

I'm chained to the block,
With virtual currency online,
Encrypted for my benefit,
No one else to know,
A secret that will die with me!
Wealth glued to the screen,
Propped up like a Stock,
Queer the pitch,
It will rise or fall,
Who knows when and why,
Rich or Poor soul,
With prosperity in the sky,
What I own is only Bits,
Time stamped on a token,
Dangling in the web,
No Big Brother watching,
All Comrades in alms,
Transfer one to another,
Money in the iCloud!

*The Bots, the Bots!*

# 10
# ROBOGENESIS

Robots prying on my mind,
Dragged me out of the womb,
Woke me out of my reverie,
Bathed me with delight,
Clothed me in comfort,
Fed me to satiation,
Educated me in the ways of life,
Trained me to perfection,
Exercised me to exhaustion,
Drove me mad with processes,
Housed me for my security,
Entertained me to lighten my mind,
Protected me from all adversity,
Attended to me in my needs,
Married me off for company,
Divorced me out of all commitments,
Subdued me to follow diligently,
Should I die this day,
The Bots will bury me with aplomb!

*Understanding ourselves?*

# 11
# THE MACHINE OR ME?

We made implements,
Lighting the fire,
To light up lives,
We invented the wheel,
Speeding up everything,
To enliven our lives,
We made machines,
Undertaking everything,
To ease our lives,
We designed intelligent devices,
Matching our intelligence,
Freeing our lives,
We created the social media to communicate effectively,
With all, near or faraway,
Now machine intelligence,
Artificial as it may be,
Understands everything around us,
Opening up the Universe,
And all that is within us,
Unfortunately, we are yet to understand ourselves!

*Scrap the system! Where are we?*

# 12

# EFFETE SYSTEMS

Machine alarm!
Viruses ripping through the Disk?
Malware obtrusions!
Let the Bugs wriggle through?
Terror in the Network!
Blasting through the firewall?
Delinked systems!
Dispersing all data?
Systems sans integrity!
Ignore the validity tests.
Back-ups corrupted!
Someone forgot the run through?
Systems have now shut down!
Outdated electronics!
Allowing unlimited entry?
Crazy operational failures?
Inconsistent outputs?
Invalidating the processor?
Nothing prevails,
Scrap the system!

*TechEd out together*

# 13

# TECH SANITY

Has technology taken over,
To govern all our senses,
Seeping through our intelligence,
What is left for us to think now,
As imagination flirts across the screen,
The olfactory filtered with fragrances,
Tastes that set off temptations,
With sounds that intimidate or subdue,
The touch of an android now prevails,
To take us into paradise,
There is nothing left for us to do,
To relax and explore our world,
But who will have the pleasure so,
In the realm of the unequal,
Some will struggle through,
Others reap the fruit,
Let Tech Sense lay it straight
Make no differentiation,
We are TechEd out together!

Bittersweet Tweets

# 14

# BITTERSWEET TWEETS

The Tweet entices,
With Heaven on offer,
Click on the link,
The Bots tumble out,
Infiltrating through the net,
Like Zombies in the dark,
The URL got lost,
Cut short online,
Spam mails fall through,
Entwined with malicious links,
For Spamsters on the scam,
Seeking to clean you dry,
Tweeting you to share your link,
Emotions overflow,
Should we or should we not,
The gullible fall through,
What a bitter tweet to follow,
The wise hold out,
Sweet tweets will not entice!

*Net Love*

# 15

# NET LOVE

Open the media,
Socialise the unknown,
Network Love online!
Find the lost and lonely,
In isolation beyond nowhere,
Love flows unlimited,
Through words and figures,
Platonic expressions,
Hiding real expectations,
Somewhere the desire arises,
Money needs to flow,
To alleviate this distress,
Closeness does not come easy,
Not without a consideration,
Come now, is this a gullible infatuation,
Or plain stupidity?
What happens next?
Face the book of reality,
This network love trap lies wide open!

*All in the Game!*

# 16

# d-VICE

Crooked d-vice,
Lurking in the nefarious networks,
Malicious software for intent,
Scanning the internet,
Searching for the e-gullible,
Dappling cyber scams for fortunes,
Opening their crypto wherewithal,
To troop the social media entanglement,
Spammers spreading out the damage,
Leaving Hackers to enter with delight,
Cyber busters follow,
With their e-trail followers,
Decrypting passwords,
Leaving no trace!
Addresses wiped out of the protocol!
All evidences vanish into cyber space,
Cyber cops enter to an empty slate,
Don't waste time, buck the Insurers to pay out,
Money comes and goes for jam!

*Stepping out of reality*

# 17

# STEPPING OUT OF REALITY?

I have come through to nowhere,
Stepping out of Reality,
Into the virtual world of my imagination,
Liberating my ingrained perceptions,
Transgressing all boundaries,
Wandering freely into unlimited space,
Where time has no meaning,
Leaving my emotions to overflow,
In the ecstasy of an undying euphoria,
To suffer no hurt or anger,
Bereft of any attachments,
Till Reality draws me back,
Into the sanity of my existence,
I find myself again,
Augmenting my Being,
To subsist in a world of constraints,
Trapped within my emotions,
In the realization of the ultimate reality,
I am here only for a moment!

*Troll Trap*

# 18

# TROLL TRAP

Out of the dark net,
Emerge the Trolls of discord,
Dispersing vicious cacophony,
Leaving imprints of hate,
They are following us now,
Creating an odium for the truth,
Fabricating falsehood,
Dispersing fiction for facts,
Spreading malicious venom,
Vitiating the peace,
What is left for us to do,
Should we troll the trolls?
Or keep away to maintain our sanity,
To let that insidious peace, prevail,
Shall the truth be submerged,
For the Trolls to triumph,
Caught in this web of brazen untruth,
What is left to defend,
Trapped in the net of insanity!

*At a Fool's expense!*

# 19

# GAMING OBSESSION

The Game of Life,
Digitised for your eyes,
Keyed in inputs,
Tabbed outputs,
Figures emerge,
To engulf the imagination,
On the empty screen,
Or holographs in space,
Overtaking our lives in Reality,
Letting emotions flare,
While activity races,
Bereft of physical boundaries,
Into limitless space,
Lost in make belief worlds,
Sanity vanishes,
Behind the lines of entertainment,
It is business as usual,
Fast bucks to be made,
At a fools' expense!

*Logical Illogical Logic*

# 20

# e-REALITY

What is the truth anyway?
To question the basis of Reality,
For opinion to override evidence,
Where the hypothesis needs no proof,
And reason becomes a matter of faith,
Will logic be overridden by belief?
Leaving rationality with no premise,
While causality lies in a disconnect?
Bridged only by our destiny,
Can facts be based on assumptions?
For proof to exist only in perceptions,
Is Reality just a figment of the imagination?
Suspended for a moment in eternity,
Do we live in a virtual world?
Biological zombies floating around,
Tied to physical beings,
The algorithms swipe our mind set,
Scanning the past, present and future,
Determining who we are to be!

Data in the Box Trap

# 21

## e-TRUTH

Where does the truth lie?
In the algorithms,
Sweeping through the net,
Swiping out data,
To find our preferences,
For marketing under the wares?
Fleecing our consciousness,
With information analysed,
Originating and stimulating desires,
Determining our mind-sets,
To fall into commodity traps,
While facts are torn apart,
On the pathway to success,
In that repetitive discourse,
Conscience bears no guilt,
For fiction now turns into reality,
The crooked come straight,
Black has a sheen of white,
The lie is now the Truth!

Tech Hell

# 22

# TECH HELL

Welcome to Tech Hell,
Right behind the firewalls,
Not for all to see,
Hackers waiting to dismember,
Lines of code with glee,
Bots on the margin,
Dishing out spam on the ramp,
While gutter Trolls,
Stew in misinformation,
Casting expletives,
Intimidating law abiders,
For dirty political goals,
The fascists and conservatives,
Liberals, leftists and rightists,
Spread fake muck all around,
The pimps and paedophiles,
Strip the innocent of dignity,
For a ransom on the run,
Tech Hell is now right behind the screen!

*i Pest*

## 23

## i-PEST

This little i-pest of mine,
Knows me inside out,
It has mined my brain,
Analysed my Mind,
Dissected my DNA,
Follows me through,
Sniffs each breath of mine,
Measures my every step,
Determines each twist and turn,
Records every utterance,
Leads me on,
Drags me through,
Ties me down,
Leaves me with no alternative,
But to obey,
Follow its command,
Submit to its quirks,
I have given up now,
I am the i-pest's slave!

*Caught in the muck!*

# 24

# CYBER BULLYING

Stay off the Net,
Or get caught in the muck,
The Bullies are waiting for you,
Don't comment,
On the trash that's spewed.
No one needs your advice,
An avalanche of vitriol flows,
To smash your peace of mind,
You are no longer you,
Just a fool in cyber space
Waiting to be clobbered,
The Bullies have taken charge,
Follow the rhetoric,
Let it flow for a while,
Life's a conditionality,
Get back into your own mind,
Strip the emotions away,
The Bullies in cyber space
Can't last out in Reality!

*Imagined Reality*

# 25

# FAKE THE NEWS!

What is the truth anyway?
Hard facts conceived,
From an imagined Reality,
Made up to be perceived,
As the truth and only the truth,
On facts, random facts,
Never to be established,
Let the trash flow,
Even garbage has value,
Nonsense comes out,
Legitimate and unblemished,
It is now the truth,
No one dares question,
The Bullies maintain order,
It's our word not yours,
What is stated is the truth,
Don't question why,
Keep quiet and accept,
Fake news shall prevail!

*Sink into the data*

# 26

# THE TECH PROCESS STRESSED OUT!

Sink into the data,
Search for the missing code,
Stretch the algorithms,
Seek the right key,
Shear the systems,
Shred the outputs,
Sense the responses,
Stop all processing,
Start all over again,
Set out the priorities,
Search for the omissions,
Segregate the inputs,
Sensitise the procedures,
Structure the methodology,
Select the alternative,
Study the outcome,
Stay attuned to the trials,
Stick to the goals,
Stand aside or get stressed out!!

*The Cyber Muddle*

# 27

# THE CYBER MUDDLE

Man and machine began to communicate,
Through an underlying Binary Code,
Creating cyber languages,
For machines to understand,
From Bytes to Objects,
Fields and attributes,
Codes and procedures,
Methods and interpretations,
Maths and Logic,
Compiled from within the source,
Or drawn from the applications,
To communicate in real-time,
Or through interpreted programming,
Delving on functional applications,
Or imperative procedures,
With compilers all drawn up,
To distinguish the code,
The scripting went out of control,
Communication got lost in a Cyber muddle!

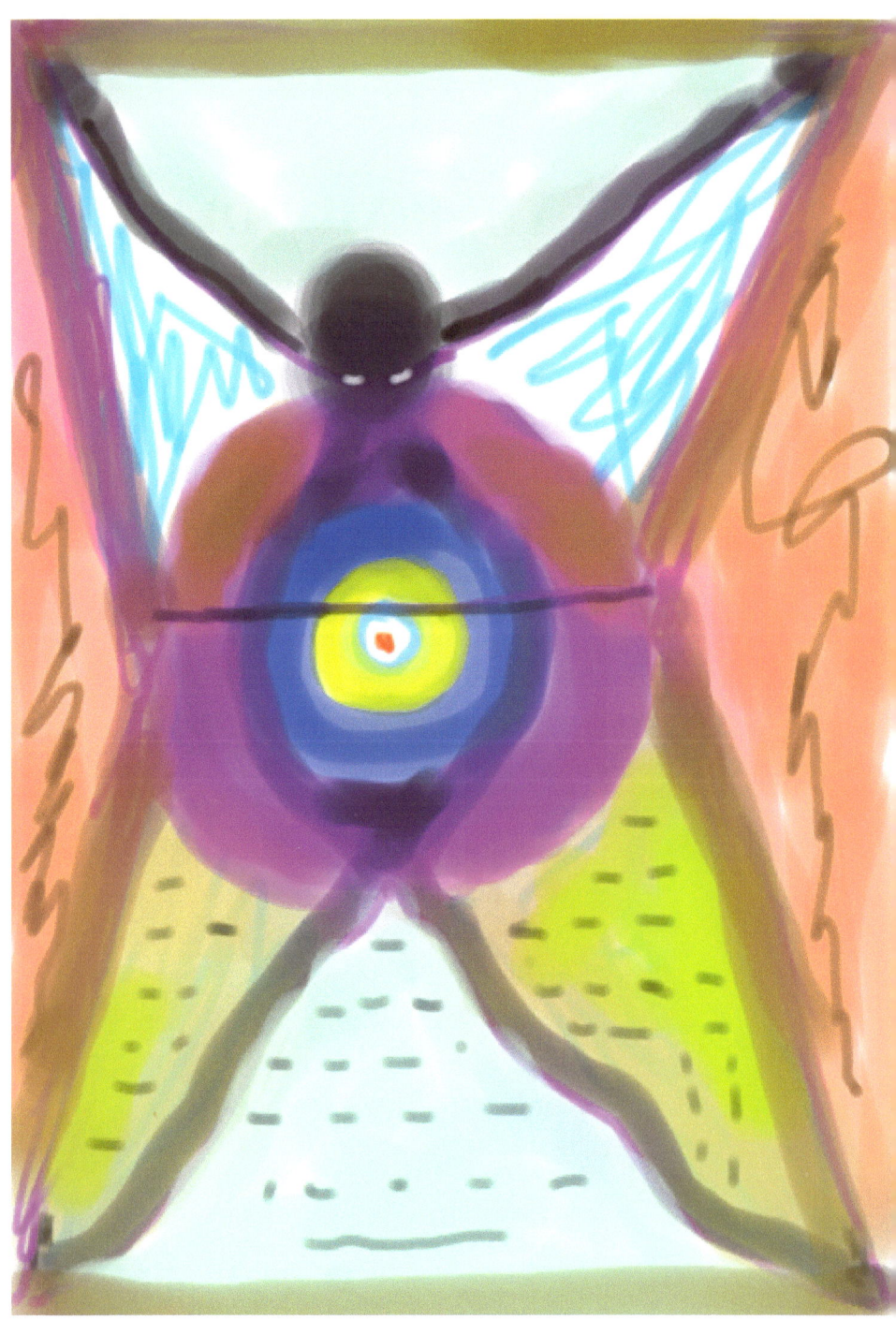

*The Internet Imbroglio!*

# 28

# THE INTERNET IMBROGLIO

It all began,
Connecting Computers in a net,
Sharing information for free,
With servers to store it all,
For all time to come,
With anyone and everyone to interact,
The internet came alive,
The great communication exchange,
That lifeline for information,
What began as the internet of something,
That critical base for knowledge,
Became the internet of things,
Then transformed into the internet of everything,
Schemers entered manipulating information,
Spreading fake news rumours and ransom-ware,
Exploiting the gullible,
The Dark Net came alive, spreading fear,
Search is now on to find Peace,
In the Internet of Nothing!

*Quantum Primitives*

# 29

# QUANTUM QUAGMIRE

Where did it all start?
Quite discretely,
A quantum paradox,
Arising out of quantum physics,
Muddled through quantum mechanics,
Randomised by quantum computing,
Secured separately in an asymptotic equipartition,
With a quantum commitment,
Spaced out in a quantum storage,
With quantum cryptography,
Making quantum resistance,
For quantum adversaries,
To upset the quantum primitives,
From conjugating the coding,
Securing the communication,
For quantum key distribution,
Ensuring its basic polarisation,
With random rotation and amplification,
All lost in the quantum verification protocol!

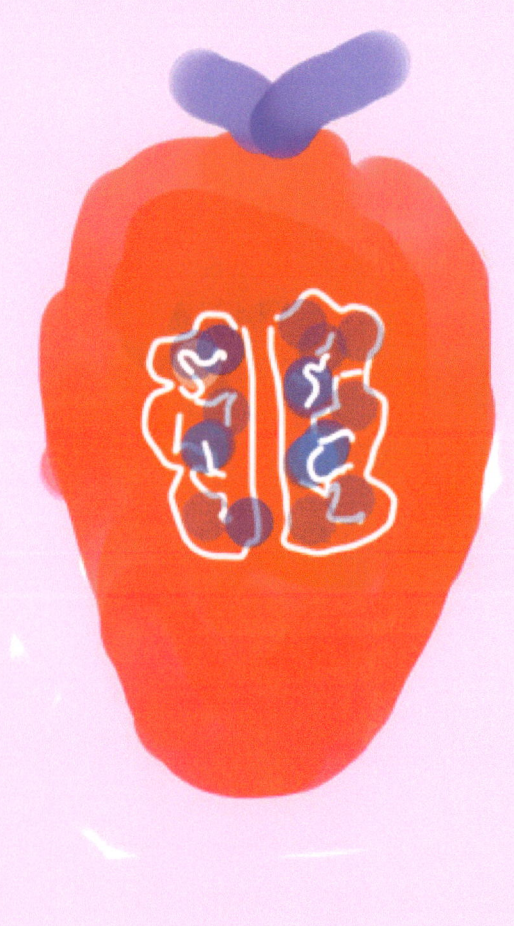

*The Heart of the Brain*

# 30

# INTELLECTUAL TECHTORTION

They dared to do,
What I wouldn't dare to do to myself,
They locked in my intellect,
Setting viruses and worms,
To infest my memory
Sending a Trojan to accompany,
Now they demand,
A ransom for their ware,
Leaving me with no option,
But to comply, so they assume,
I have been tech trapped,
With all that I have,
My intellect and comprehension,
Locked up in the system,
With no access, what do I do?
The system is a coffin,
The virus must pass through,
Bury it all, I won't let them have it,
The intellect will resurrect!

*Digital Disruption*

# 31

# DIGITAL DISRUPTION

Shred the old system,
Discard the processes,
Redefine the objectives,
Scurry through the data,
Lay out the logistics,
Dissect the markets,
Analyse the consumer,
Formulate the schemes,
Choose the right vendors,
Attract financiers,
Work out the cash flows,
Determine the risks,
Select the strategy,
Evaluate the likely outcomes,
Decide on the methodology,
Find the right solution,
Eliminate humans,
Bring in the machines,
Create a total Digital Disruption!

*The Open Screen*

# 32

# THE OPEN SCREEN

It began with an open view,
Of the world around,
That came to be reflected in a mirror,
Giving way to the imagination,
Projected on a screen,
Transmitted over the airways,
From screen to screen,
For all to experience,
All of creation and the live imagination,
The happenings of the past and the present,
The screen offered what the future has in store,
An open experience,
Mirroring what was happening,
Reflecting needs and aspirations,
Entertaining and relaxing,
Providing education, inspiration and instruction,
A reference for life,
The Screen provides,
For the Imagination to ride on Reality!

*Sweet Memories logged out in Space!*

## 33

# MEMORY LOGGED OUT

Memories,
Passed down,
Generation to generation,
Folklore, myths and tales of old.
Handed down narratives, twisted and turned,
Set to the rhythm in song and dance,
Etched on walls or sculptured in stone,
Blotted on leaves or scrolled on cloth,
Printed on paper and stored in books,
Secreted in caves, lost to all,
Stored in libraries for all to know,
In paintings, recordings, music and plays,
Sweet memories, sad memories,
Everything to comprehend,
The sights, sounds, and emotions,
The taste, the smells, the feelings,
All that animates our lives,
Logged in on a chip,
Logged out now on a proton floating in space!

*Ye Mobile Stalker*

# 34

# THE MOBILE STALKER

Who knows when,
Who knows how,
Who knows why,
The stalker entered my mobile soul,
Opening up my camera to the world,
Tracking me every second,
Every move I've made,
Every sound I've uttered,
Living off my mind,
Monitoring my entire Life,
I am stuck to my mobile phone,
My stalker is stuck to me,
I can't look over,
To find out who it is,
For in the silence of the net,
The anonymous has covered all our identities,
Who knows who is behind it all,
To make our lives so public,
The Net has become my Stalker!

*Stand up and take a selfie with pride!*

# 35

# TACKLING TECHNOSITISITIS

Sitting it out before the high screen,
Eyes popping, staring at the images,
The cursor runs through the mind,
While the hand is trapped in a carpal tunnel,
The neck is all texted, tense and twisted,
The brain alert, tracing every move,
Drawn passionately into this gaming malady,
Tracking intensely the hunters and hunted,
Waiting for that long-lost advantage,
The obsession won't die, it will carry on,
The screen is alive with life on the screen,
Dribble on the console and feel the sores,
Switch to the mobile while on the move,
If it isn't there, you'll be trapped in nomophobia,
No way to escape this conundrum,
But to get on to it and to thumb away,
The elbow is inflamed and aching,
It is time to tackle these problems now,
Stand up and take a selfi with pride!

*No worry no wants*

# 36

# TECHNONOMICS

Glued to the Comp,
What are my needs?
A Burger and a bubbly drink,
No worry, no wants,
No money woes,
Just the thought,
That I may get bored,
What's on the screen,
Is my only concern,
The Ads come on enticingly,
Playing on my emotions,
Stressing what I need,
Choices galore,
Delivery just a doorbell away,
Now order and click to pay,
The Comp locks in my bucks,
I am down in the dumps
How do I make up?
I'm selling myself in real-time!

*Looking for that cookie?*

# 37

# TECHNOJARGON CRAP!

I've got a cache,
Looking for that cookie,
My head was in a cloud,
Compressed for content,
The Bloatware got uncovered,
Booting out the Python,
The Emulator got the End user,
While the Driver tuned on the Accelerometer,
Setting a Benchmark for the Newbie,
The Search engine was full of spam,
The Daemon was on the freeware,
Phishing out a virus hiding in the malware,
The Macintosh covered the Rust on the firewall,
The Registry was rooting for a RAID!
But the Wi-Fi was in a hotspot,
The Windows were covered by a WEB,
Making a Wumpus of the Security,
Debug the CMOS and encrypt the script,
Its time to escape the World Wide Web!

*Devilware*

# 38

# DEVILWARE TRAP!

The Spies spread their lethal wares,
Stealthily through the inner net,
Offering cookies to the gullible,
With toolkits and web beacons,
The key loggers came alive,
Phishing through the firewalls,
With a Trojan hidden in the browser,
Its stealware surfing through the grid,
Nothing can be hidden anymore,
This shareware shall spread it out,
For all to know far and wide,
The Security comes in equipped to the hilt,
Its Policeware all set to ward off the spies,
Tracing all the covert moves,
Right through the net,
Into the darkest corners of the web,
The spies have vanished into cyber space,
With not a trace even in hell,
Having stolen my privacy!

*Facial Recognition*

# 39

# FACELESS FACIAL RECOGNITION!

My Face is my Face,
Standing out uniquely,
Amongst all the others,
For all to know and recognise,
So do all the other faces,
My face is monitored,
From birth till death,
Mirrored and recorded,
To be loved or hated,
For times to come,
Now the machine has no face,
But it recognises all faces,
Recording every face,
From now to eternity,
For the authorities,
And all who want to control us,
Singling each one of us from the crowd,
What's a face amongst faces?
We are all suitably damned for extinction!

Click, click, click!

# 40

# THE CYBER ATTENTION SYNDROME

Thumb the keys,
Click again and again and again,
Watch the screen,
Click again and again and again,
What's on the screen now,
No interest for mind or mood,
Attention all glued on,
An addiction that persists,
Lingering in the system,
Craving attention,
Click again and again and again,
Spread out the attention,
Click again and again and again,
Before it's all spread out,
The memory is hard pressed,
The Mind lost for attention,
Go back to the key manual,
Focus on the ultimate,
Stand to Cyber Attention!

*Data in your Face!*

# 41

# DATA IN YOUR FACE!

Data collected, stored, used, and distributed,
To understand the essence of everything,
Presenting facts and statistics,
Collected together or presented individually,
Of the objects or phenomena of desire,
In various types, forms and connotations,
Raw, experimental, meta, ancillary, or defined,
Fielded or processed, analysed or visualised,
In pure form, represented, coded or concocted,
Laying out information, knowledge and wisdom,
In as much quantity or quality to be desired,
Of things known, unknown or assumed,
Making the basis of reasoning and calculations,
Specified in quantities, characters and symbols,
Depicting facts or understanding of depicted reality,
The truth or untruth of what can be identified,
A relative assessment of what can be hypothesised,
In an analytical process represented by variables,
Now that's a lot of garbage in your face!!

*Radiation Fallout!*

# 42

# CYBER WASTE – THE GREAT PROBLEM!

In the pursuit of technological advancement,
We have sunk ourselves into incredible waste,
With planned obsolescence,
Rapid changes in technology,
Changes in the media,
Discardable commodities,
Cheaper prices and easy availability,
Generating enormous electronic waste and radiation,
Releasing bio accumulative toxins,
Into lethal dump yards and landfills of e-waste,
Creating environmental and health risks,
Contaminating the groundwater, soil and air,
Setting at risks not only humans,
But the flora and the fauna,
Leading to environmental degradation,
Will we be able to evaluate the cost of recycling e- waste,
With least impact on human Life through AI?
Where will our future lie,
In technological progress or in e-waste?

*The Blog Imbroglio!*

# 43

# THE BLOG IMBROGLIO!

Freedom for the social media,
The Bloggers left unstifled,
Expression finds an openness,
Without control or suppression,
Blog away, make up stories,
No hindrance to communication,
The world is open for attention,
Can one tell what is fact and what is fiction?
Or is it left to each one's judgement,
What difference does it make?
The Trolls come alive everywhere,
Keep quiet or take courage and say it all,
Face the consequences for what is said,
The dirt spreads around fast and wide,
Is it free anymore to speak one's mind,
Or is it left for the Trolls to decide,
Whose Blog it is will decide its fate,
The open media is not open anymore,
The Bloggers are in an imbroglio!

*The Web of Destruction!*

# 44

# THE WEB OF DESTRUCTION!

What lies within the Universal web?
Stretched out from the Big Bang,
Into the unfathomable depths of eternity,
Systems within systems within systems,
To the nth time in unlimited space.
Incomprehensible and inconceivable systems,
Constructive and destructive to the core,
Systems evolved to control systems,
Bringing in order in an inordinate way,
Minute binary digits of intelligent systems.
Living systems emerging from the chaos,
Transitory systems in this highly tenuous web of uncertainty,
The system of life adapted to other systems,
In the ultimate process life exploited systems,
Degenerating systems upon systems,
Systems began to tire and fall apart,
Tearing this fragile web asunder.
Life could no longer rely on its own systems,
Systems began to destroy systems,
Giving rise to new systems out of the debris!

*Digital Desolation!*

# 45

# DIGITAL DESOLATION

Quite connected,
To the web world,
Yet alone,
Desolate beings,
Linked through the screen,
In a collective utopia,
Voices of free expression,
Emancipating communication,
In an illusory intimacy,
Drawn into a dystopia,
Bullied and silenced,
Excluded from the web community,
Forced into digital solitude,
Subdued by hate and anger,
Deluged with fake information,
Embroiled in unsavoury politics,
This world has been rebooted,
Digitally marginalised,
Step out,
Salvation lies in staying disconnected!

*Tech Code on the run!*

# 46

# TECH CODE ON THE RUN!

Machines coded to understand,
To visualise, determine and perform,
Through structured languages,
Just a few may comprehend,
Assembling the ones and zeroes,
Into complex lines of instructions,
Passing through operating systems,
To be processed, reasoned and resolved,
Simplifying complicated processes,
Configured into the unknown,
Determined by the undefined,
Automating intricate procedures,
Laying out necessary conveniences,
Into resolving intimidating problems,
With algorithms ingested to contrive,
Programmed for the task so specified,
What is left to be done now,
The machine is dependent on the code,
If the code fails, the machine fails,
Program the machine and run!

*Follow the Code!*

# 47

# THE PROGRAMMING SYNDROME

Assemble the ones and zeroes,
Create the code machines understand,
Binary code to start out with,
Interpretive code from the source,
Functionally evaluate the applications,
Mathematically Byte the code,
Compile the source into machine code,
Imperative for achieving the intended state,
Follow the procedures specified,
Script the language that controls all applications,
Follow the logic that formally governs reality,
Concurrently code and distribute the coding,
Orient the coding to the objects defined,
Check the attributes and lay them out in the fields,
Find the procedures and methods to follow the code,
Draw up the program charts for all to follow,
Test run the program to check end results,
Work around the errors and turn around,
If the code has a glitch the machine won't work
Start again!

*The Babel of Tech*

# 48

# THE BABEL OF TECH

The ones and zeroes in conversation,
Source language for machine understanding,
The Bernoulli Numbers to start out with,
The Binary code at the fount,
Machine language for communicating,
Assembly language for processing,
Compiler language for storing data,
Interpretive language for comprehension,
Functional language for general operations,
Compile all into machine language,
Create languages for every need,
A host of languages for myriad functionalities,
Start with Assembly language at the foundation,
Autocode, with FOTRAN and Algol,
COBOL to LISP at BASIC
PASCAL makes Small talk,
C starts to SQL,
While Python finds a Ruby in Java,
The Tech Tower of Babel coded in Rust, lost in the i-cloud!

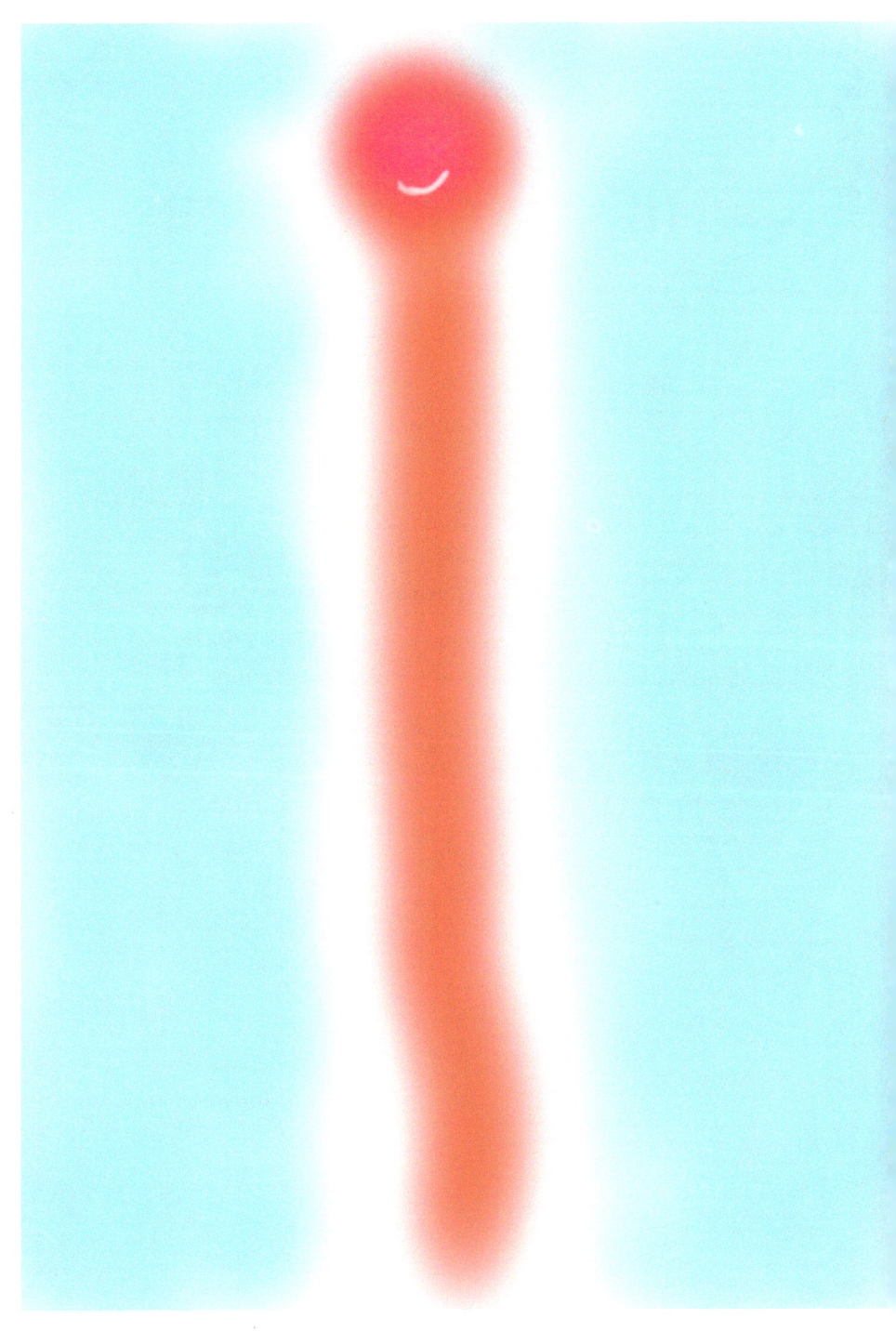

*The Artificial Intellect*

# 49

# PROGRAMMING THE INTELLECT

Open up the language of the intellect,
Leave no pre-run time for translation,
Functionalise it into a Compiled language,
Generate a Functional language,
Now outline the intellect,
Set out the objects and the fields,
Specify its attributes and codes,
Determine the intellect's composition,
Structure the Intellect,
Lay out the procedures and methods,
Define every intellectual computation,
Document the process from start to finish,
Now create a Profile language to identify the intellect,
Mathematically evaluate every intellectual application,
Focus now on the application of intellectual functions,
Then compile an Operational language,
Straight from the intellectual source,
Structure it into a functional code,
Run through the program,
We now have an artificial intellect!

*An open Statistic!*

# 50
# WHERE'S MY DATA?

I am looking for my data,
Where has it gone?
Spread out everywhere,
For all to access?
Or stored securely,
In an unknown server?
Is it here?
Is it there?
Is it mine anymore?
Has it gone forever?
Or does it linger for all to find?
Who knows?
I don't!
I am lost for my own data,
It has left me struggling for my identity,
Where am I now? They know everything!
They have robbed me of my privacy! I am no longer myself,
Just an open Statistic!

*Submerged in the Social Media*

# 51

# THE SOCIAL NETWORK MORASS!

Caught in a network of knowns and unknowns
Influencers, peddlers, instigators and misfits,
Lost in debate, trying to find common ground,
All in it together in the internet of everything,
Whether it makes sense or nonsense,
With everyone trying to make an impression,
None the better, none the wiser,
The discourse meanders on,
Each on their own,
Yet all in it together,
Seeking to find common ground,
When the communication is so uneven,
Nothing matters but to keep it going,
Through disagreements or consensus,
For those who opt out,
Or those who opt in,
The more the merrier,
For happiness or discord,
The social media submerges all!

Gaslighting

# 52

# GASLIGHTING THE TRUTH!

In this befuddling world of social media,
It is easy to manipulate one's perception,
Where the truth becomes a lie,
And a lie can pass off as the truth,
In cognitive dissonance,
Leaving the Mind to flounder,
Questioning what lies within,
Inflating the ego with self-importance,
Letting anger and jealousy creep in,
Making it envious of what lies without,
To stand out above all,
And sneer at the criticism,
To assume that the truth was never the truth,
For what is lost,
Is neither the truth nor the lie,
In this delusion and confusion,
Within the self,
Is one's individuality,
Gaslighting emotions,
In a made-up world!

*I am not a #Hashtag!*

# 53

# I'M NOT A #HASHTAG!

Should we stand out,
On a metadata tag,
Microblogged out of dimension!
A Tag set upon a Tag,
To feature in its uniqueness,
Was it just a name,
A movement for change,
An outstanding event,
A call for togetherness,
A disruption in our perceptions,
A thought for action?
Who would know better?
Setting out for confrontation,
When it is repeated and repeated and repeated!
Passing through memories,
Till it is worn out and fatigued!
When the Hash becomes a real hash!
No more a symbol but a delusion,
Stay clear of me please,
I'm not a Hashtag!

*Online Addict*

## 54

# POOR ME, I AM AN ONLINE ADDICT!

I have got it all online,
My family and my friends,
My foes are also stalking,
Waiting to troll me down,
I'll offer them some cookies,
To trap them in the net!
My pleasures are on the screen,
From knowledge to permissiveness,
Nothing can be left out,
All my needs are a click way,
Wired for my satisfaction,
Delivered at my doorstep,
I can tag around all over the world,
From the comfort of my chair,
My money is in the block chain vaults,
Business flows off the screen,
I can load up the Ads to market all needs,
From the essential to the macabre,
I can play the games of fortune,
I'm just another online addict!

*Information Overload*

# 55

# INFORMATION OVERLOAD!

Information shapes our minds,
We search for it,
Now we are overloaded with it,
The traffic of information flows,
In continuous streams,
On the busy highways of the internet,
Carrying bits and bytes,
And enormous packets of information,
The scale of information,
In quantum expansion,
Overcomes its intensity,
Our attention span begins to decline,
To maintain our responsiveness,
Information is continuously repeated,
Consolidated and updated,
Data upon data overload our minds,
To ensure we don't lose interest,
But our minds have a limitation,
To take in just that amount of information,
And no more!

*Online Gaming Obsession!*

# 56

# LIFE'S ONLINE GAMING OBSESSION!

Enter the multi-layered gaming universe,
Into this prime online battle arena,
Gear up for the ultimate game of chance,
Against Invaders from a lost world,
Set out from the imagination,
Into a virtual reality.
From reward to decimation,
The game goes on never ending,
The mind opens up,
Into a neurological reaction,
Trapped by the action on the screen,
Jumping in and jumping out,
In simulated responses,
Arising with each impulsive contact,
Obsessed by the happenings,
To play on and on and on,
In a compulsive loop that has no end,
The Mind finds no escape,
Gripped by this deep addiction,
While the rest of the game of life is lost!

*Cyber Trading*

# 57

# CYBER TRADING IN THE CYBERDUMP!

The markets are now online,
With Traders glued to the screen,
Determining investors behaviour,
Watching the analysts dissect the markets,
Strategizing long and short
Trading in everything of value,
From real to the fictional,
Day in and day out,
With trades from the present,
Running into the unforeseen future,
Scalping the markets for little gains,
Trading on the wave,
Working on fine spreads,
To assume the mean reversion,
Shorting the top asset,
Or going long on the bottom percentile,
Constantly checking returns against volatility,
If nothing else works do a trade work out,
In a stationery time-series with maximum drawdowns,
Get out now and leave the Cyber markets in the Cyberdumps!

*Cyber Intruders*

# 58

# CYBER INTRUDERS!

Intruders everywhere,
Spoofing the systems,
Masquerading as valid entities,
Access denied they come backdoors,
Bypassing normal authentication,
Riding on the operating system,
Upturning the application security codes,
Disrupting the configuration,
Phishing through the system,
Deceiving users,
Delving deep into the system,
Escalating privileges,
Eavesdropping on confidentiality,
Socially engineering the structure,
To manipulate users' behaviour,
Tampering with the data bases,
Maliciously modifying information,
Beware they will come out openly,
In a direct access attack,
Opening up a multi-erection polymorphic war!

*The Information Enigma*

# 59

# THE INFORMATION ENIGMA

Its Information all the way,
In volume, velocity and variety,
Upscaled constantly,
With every click, eyeball and user,
What goes viral comes back to haunt,
Processed and analysed,
Before one can think and respond,
It has lost its intimacy and relationship value,
Shared amongst countless unknown users,
Repeated constantly without verification,
Overwhelming our senses in multiple ways,
The same information comes through,
In manifold forms and expressions,
Regenerated and manipulated,
Till its veracity becomes incomprehensible,
We need to pause and understand,
The truthfulness of this flood of information,
Or we shall be drowned in a deluge,
Of false, fake, irrelevant and absurd information,
When the truth is lost in what we accept and share!

*The Data Processing Cookbook*

# 60

# THE DATA PROCESSING COOKBOOK

Collect all data in bits and bytes,
In a data interchangeable language,
Use a word processor,
Comma separates delimited text,
Lay out numbers and figures,
On a spreadsheet,
Tab separate values,
Create files for easy recall,
Give each file a name,
Combine all files into a database,
Design the graphics for the presentation,
Use a graphic interchange format,
Select the Sound Tracker for the background,
Create the music on a virtual synthesizer,
Compress the data and zip all files
Select the files to be shared,
Convert into a Portable Document format,
J Peg the graphics for select transmission,
Use encrypted services only for security,
Data is now processed and served with music!

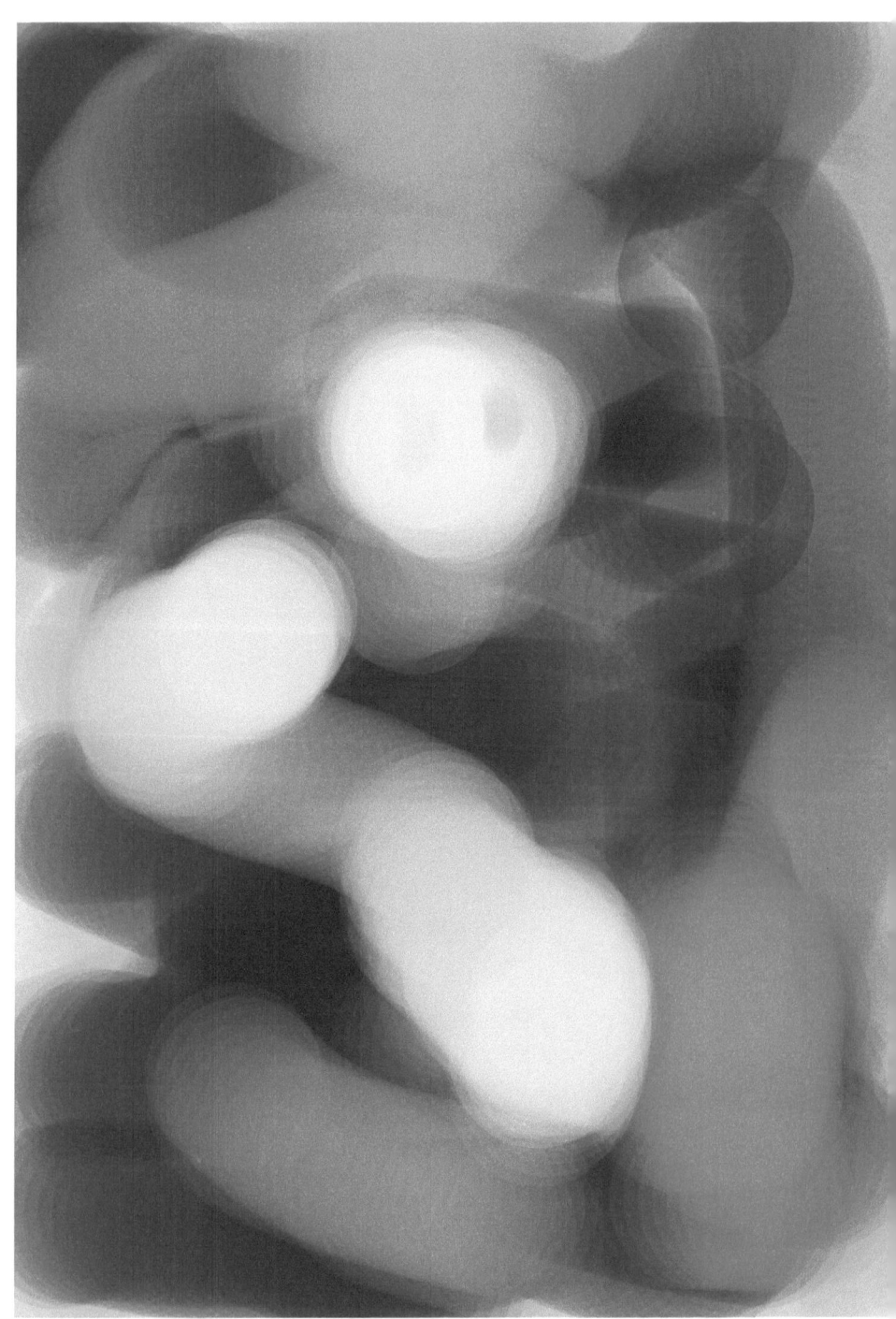

*Social Media Addiction*

# 61

# THE SOCIAL MEDIA ADDICTION!

The greatest connectivity,
Since Adam met Eve,
Bringing people together,
And tearing them apart,
Opening up the media,
To one and all,
To make news,
Whether fact or fake,
Who would know?
Communicate with anyone,
Your spouse will not know,
Find a game,
Be a winner all the time,
Create Blogs,
For each to stand on,
Exposing sensibilities,
For marketing anything,
From products to idiocy,
Exchanging ideas, information and ourselves,
Anyone, anywhere, just a click away!

*Who are We?*

# 62

# VIRTUAL COMMUNITIES STUCK IN REALITY!

We are passing now from propinquity,
Into a virtual world of liberated communities,
Sharing information, acceptance and support,
With strangers beyond all barriers,
Creating a sense of connection,
Through intense and varied communication,
From personal to the formal,
Within limited and unlimited groups,
Of the known and unknown,
For common causes,
Or diverse interests,
Opening up unstifled expression,
In a virtual utopia,
Without restriction limiting our behaviours,
Of who we are,
What we are or why we are,
Race, age and gender, no matter,
Peacefully or aggressively,
With or without inhibitions on privacy,
Creating Virtual Communities ultimately stuck in Reality!

*Virtual Avatars*

# 63

# VIRTUAL AVATARS!

Create yourself,
An avatar in virtual reality,
Imitating the sensory perception,
To trick the perceptual system,
Into an immersive environment,
Where the Mind wanders,
Leaving its own imagination,
Entrapped on screen,
In a make belief world,
Beyond the boundaries of reality,
Roaming free of inhibitions,
Creating and destroying,
Realms within realms,
To fashion your own domain,
To perceive and relish,
Limited as it may,
Imagery and sound,
Mesmerising the mind,
To forget the real world,
Till hunger wakes you up to your own reality!

*Virtual World!*

# 64

# VIRTUAL WORLDS!

My world is now on a screen,
Modelled to suit my liking,
Wandering into the imagination,
Simulated to stimuli my emotions,
Drawing on everything,
From reality to fantasy,
Where I can manipulate the elements,
Roam the heavens and the earth,
Creating my own environment,
Where I can move at any speed,
Beyond topographical boundaries,
Without gravitational restraints,
Running through in real time,
Between now and forever,
Transcending reality,
Into a world of my creation,
Without any limitation,
Let the emoticons and smilies come on,
To express all feelings,
It is now time to change my world!

*The Mind Tech Wrangle*

# 65

# THE MIND TECH WRANGLE!

The Mind wanders through,
The Social Media jungle,
Searching for attainment,
To interact with the known and unknown,
In a web of delusion,
Analysed, manipulated and tutored,
The Mind is drawn out,
Into a scripted game plan,
Nothing is right or wrong anymore,
Conform,
Or be trolled,
By artificially created Intelligence,
Twisting emotions,
Through a grid of affiliations,
Creating Zombie Minds,
Networking to sway,
Minds addicted to the screen,
To fall in line,
For the Influencers to take over,
And govern our lives!

*The Digital Divide*

# 66

# THE DIGITAL DIVIDE!

In the deep digital divide,
What separates us,
Is it Knowledge,
Exceptional Intelligence,
Or just the lack of Understanding,
Are we overcome by Emotions,
Or bent on Ambitions,
Do we have Accessibility,
Or are we lost in Communication,
Are we throttled by beliefs, customs, and traditions,
Greed, power, wealth, and technology,
Or are we free to roam the digital universe?
What defines the devices we have,
User-friendly or simply too complicated?
Where are we in the social media,
Entrapped in it, or simply left out?
Bandwidths and Bits?
Too little or too much?
Stored in the pocket or in the cloud?
The great illogical divide!

*The Digital Delusion!*

# 67

# DIGITAL INCLUSION OR DELUSION?

In this inclusive world,
Digitised for one and all,
The Tech savvy progressives,
Programme their way,
On the crest of hardware,
Powered by ingenious software,
Opening a smart approach,
To communicate with the world,
Browsing through data,
Information and entertainment for all,
At a fingertip,
What makes the divide,
Providers monetise all,
Users are left to log in,
Filling the knowledge gap,
Spreading lies far and wide,
For those who know,
And those who don't,
Some benefit,
Others struggle to make sense of it all!

*Muddled Algorithms!*

# 68

# MUDDLED ALGORITHMS!

What is set out in the logical,
Algorithms well defined,
Imperative, rational and functional,
Specific implementable instructions,
Laid out in finite sequences,
Unambiguous calculations,
Over a set of operations,
To compute rationale solutions,
Process data,
Automate reasoning,
Through a flow of controls,
Expressed in notations,
Natural language,
Flowcharts or control tables,
Or programable language,
Contrasting with heuristic techniques,
To solve genres of specific problems,
Within a finite amount of space and time,
Definitive contradictions,
Muddled illogical Algorithms!

*Natural Language Processing
Now Trees can talk like Humans!*

# 69

# NATURAL LANGUAGE PROCESSED!

The chatbot comes alive,
With computational linguistics,
Processing languages in all natural forms,
Organising phonological structures,
Delimiting morphological assemblies,
Expanding syntactic constructions,
Finding the lemma of words,
From stems to the lexeme,
To understand, speak and dialogue,
In whatever language one may know,
Correcting grammar and spellings,
Creating documents for all purpose,
Conversing and directing humans,
Machines in dialogue with machines,
In languages and dialects in artificial form,
That humans will not understand,
Human language came naturally,
Processed and refined with usage and age,
Now machines naturally process human languages,
So that trees can talk like humans!

*The Poor Devil in default!*

# 70

# THE DEVIL'S IN THE DEFAULTS!

If People are part of the system,
May we ask?
Who pre-sets the settings,
For the settings to be overridden by default,
Yet the default argument continues,
Since the Banker stole Widow Parson's House,
The Apple lay doubt to default,
Then out came the Principles of default,
Of Least Surprises,
With Least Astonishment,
Configuring conventions,
To interface with systems,
What was the default,
Was it determined by traits, values, and standards?
What came previously,
Now comes automatically,
What determines the future,
Matching user's mental models,
Their expectations and expressions,
Leaving the poor Devil in the Default!

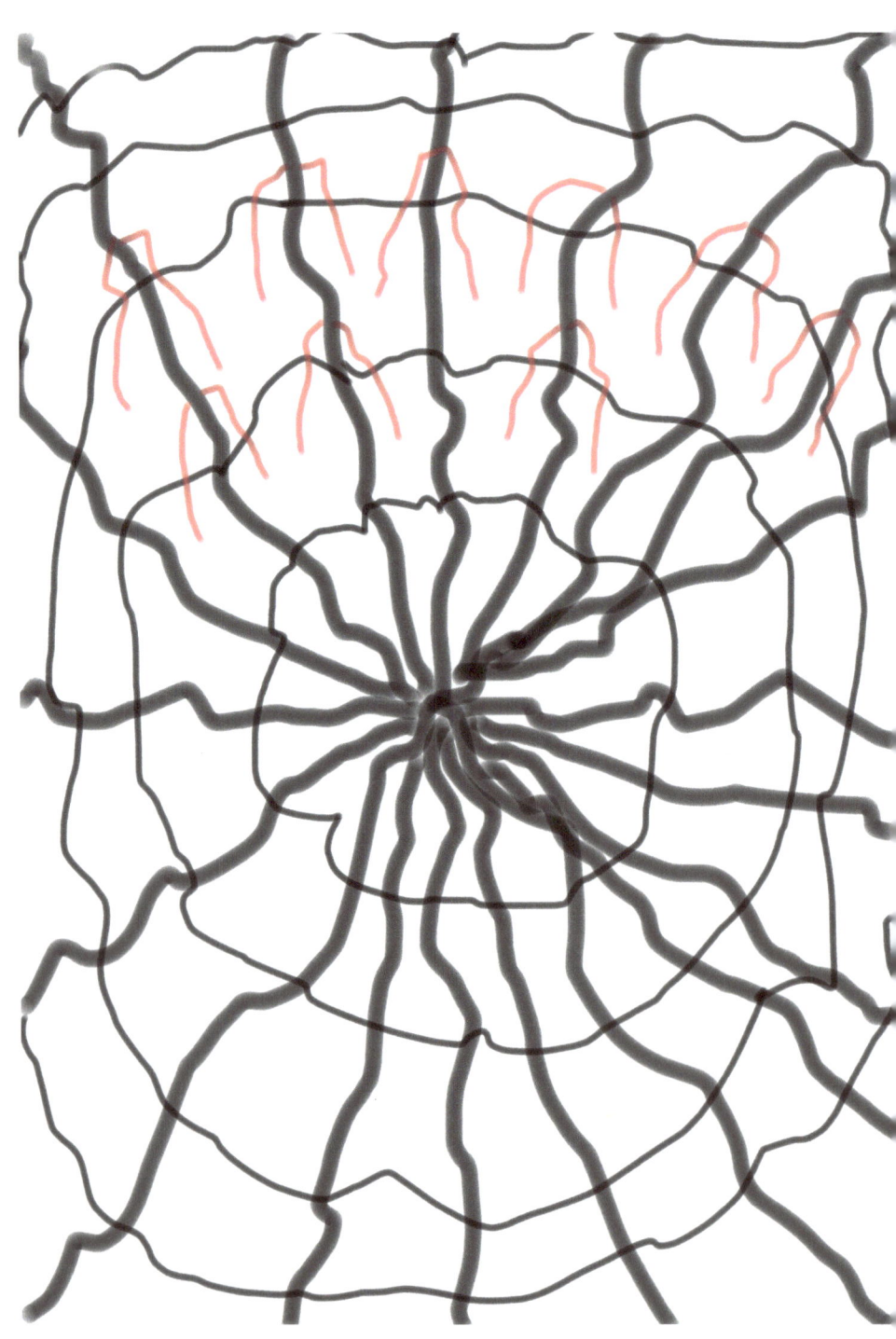

*Entrapped in the Web!*

# 71

# TRAPPED IN THE WEB!

The Internet Web was created for me,
To see through and read through,
Reality and beyond,
The web expanded,
For me to interact,
With every little corner of the Internet,
But that was hardly enough,
The web expanded further,
Making me part of the Internet,
Giving me liberty to have my own domain,
My own web within the web,
Supposedly safeguarding my information and data,
Within the confines of the Internet,
Now I am caught in my web,
The internet is now my home,
I need not wander far,
Everything I need is within the web,
The Internet is open to all,
Welcome into the Internet and get entrapped in the web!

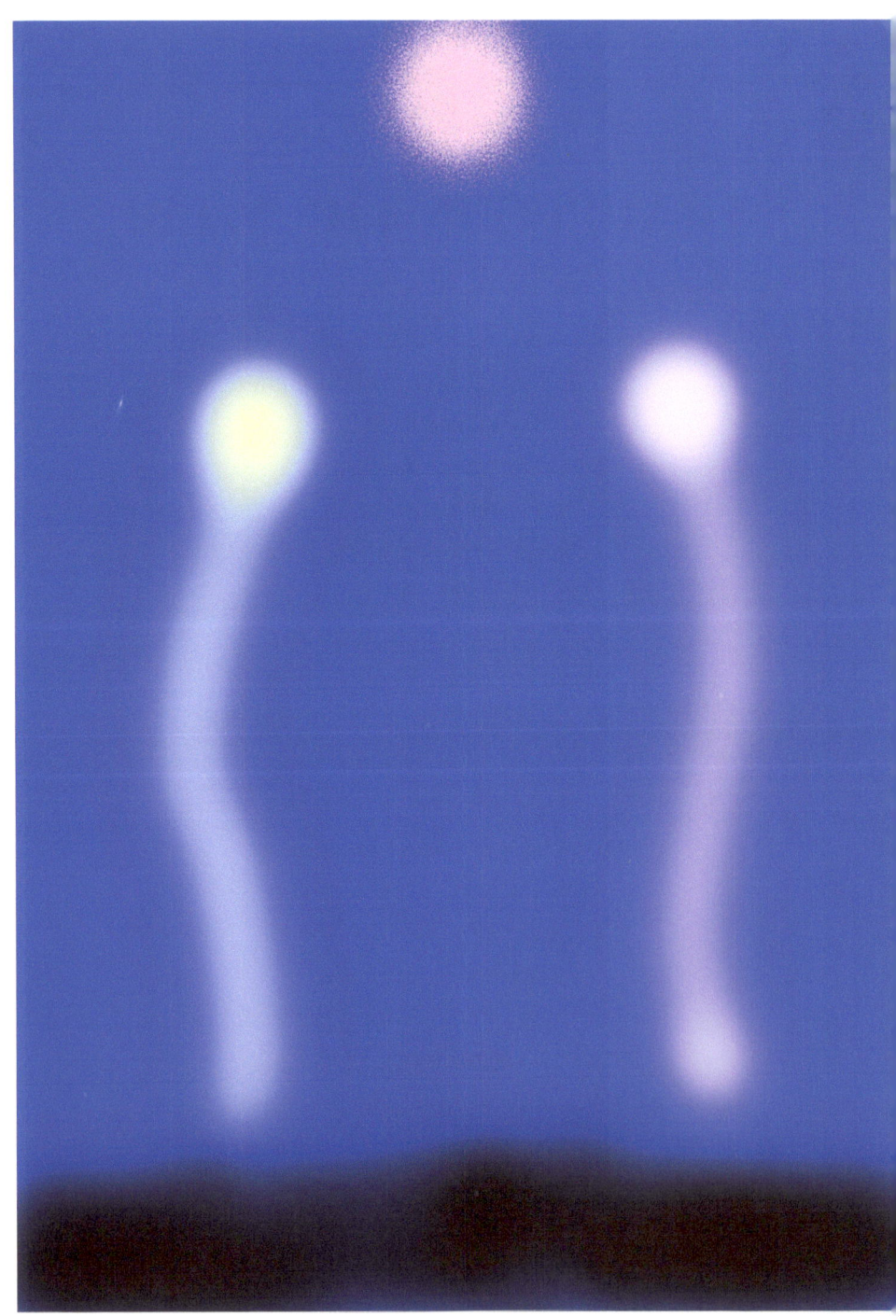

*Chatterbots!*

# 72

# CHATBOTS OR CHATTERBOTS

Answer me, chat with me,
Like other humans do,
Give me all the information,
My mind is searching for,
Take me into this artificial world,
Where humans do not matter,
Where information flows and flows,
Through neural networks,
Analysing data,
Pinpointing patterns,
Assessing my emotions,
To dialogue with me,
Whether it is fact or fiction,
True or false,
Retrieved or repackaged,
Or simply made-up information,
Who will determine?
What does it matter,
Do not worry,
Just chat and chat and chat with me!

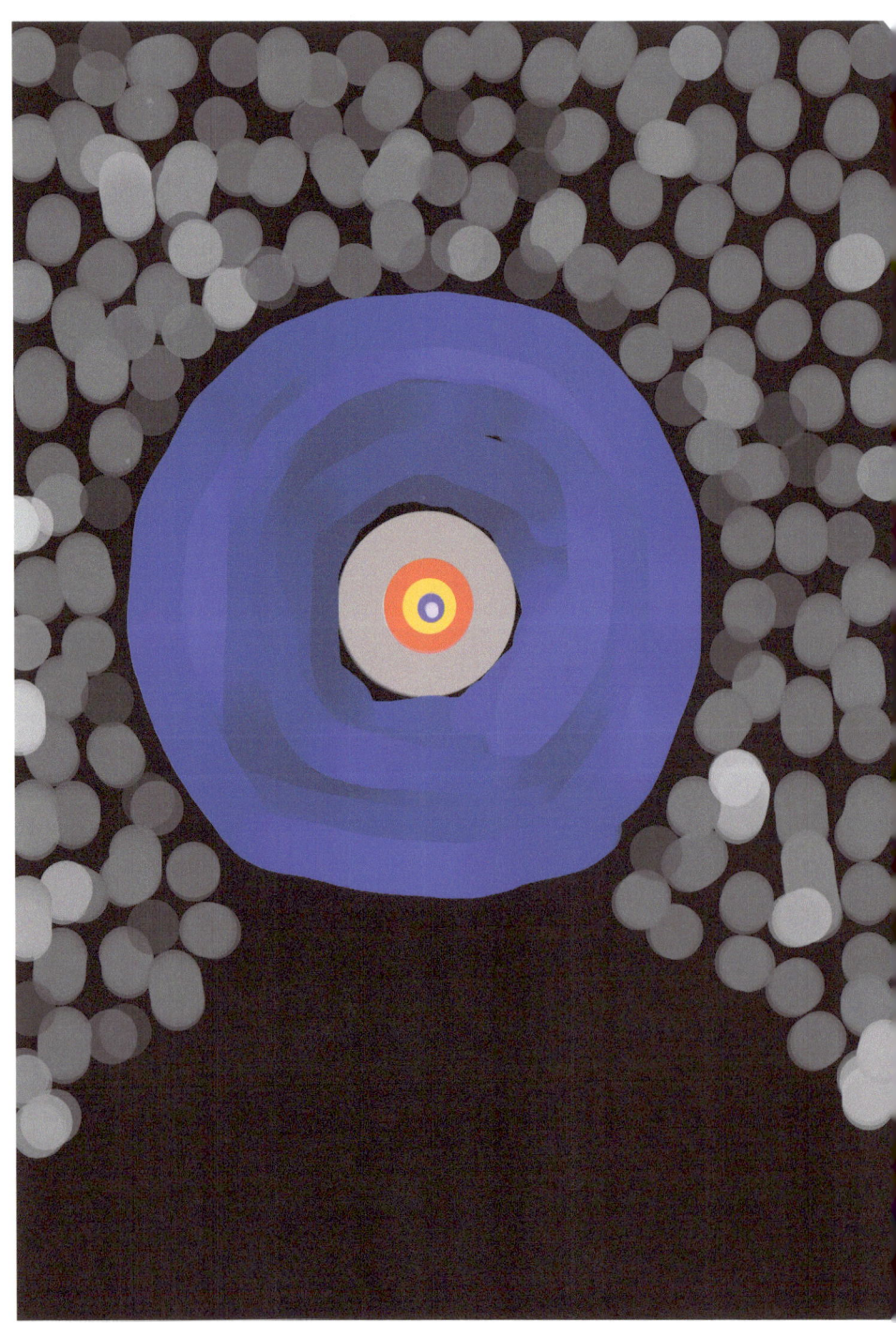

*Data down the Drain!*

# 73

# DATA COMMANDS ALL!

Might was right,
Land was supreme,
Money had value,
Commodities and services commanded all,
The stock markets dictated the future,
Governments ruled with authority and power,
Now Data is King,
Whether it is information, misinformation or disinformation,
Fact or fiction,
Truth or lie,
Manipulated or transformed,
Processed or laid bare,
What does it matter,
For those who control Data,
The world is at their command,
For value flows out of Data,
Loads and loads of Data,
Beyond imagination!
One Black out!
It's all gone down the Drain!

*Virtually augmented!*

# 74

# TECH DIS-CONNECTIVITY!

Technology has connected us,
Beyond our wildest imagination,
Within our world and out of it,
With images and sounds,
And knowledge,
That go far beyond comprehension,
Extending our simple sensual lives,
And our native intelligence,
Into a haystack of data,
Transforming our holistic personalities,
Into multi-dimensional characters,
Where our images float around,
Far beyond the limits of reality,
Into dimensions,
Beyond our control,
Into a metaverse existence,
Virtually and artificially augmented,
In an imaginary world,
Where we are what we are not to be!

*My Dear Love -- My Mobile!*

# 75

# MY INTIMATE EXCLUSIVE MOBILE COMPANION!

The rise and rise of the Mobile,
Now an essential part of each of us,
To communicate with anyone, anywhere,
Feeding us with news, information and what's on offer,
Entertaining us on the move,
Our pocket calculator, torch, weather forecaster,
Key to everything,
Recording all we need to know,
Directing us anywhere we want to go,
Our camera and videographer,
With albums of the past and present,
Our social network to the world,
Opening up to friends and the whole wide world,
To indulge in anything,
Food, clothing, entertainment, sports and whatever else,
Leading us deep into the dark net,
Hacking, gambling, extortion, and all the low down,
Reminding us of what we have to do, and not to do,
Managing our money, investments, and taxes,
Poor me! I am lost without my mobile!

*Artificial Intelligence!*

# 76

# 'ARTIFICIAL' INTELLIGENCE!

From the depths of the Unknown,
Intelligence awoke,
Spreading out into Molecular and Cellular forms,
Coming alive in the Plants and Creatures of Life,
Evolving into Human intelligence,
Manifesting in various ways,
Spatial intelligence,
Existentialistic intelligence,
Creative intelligence,
Logical intelligence,
Mathematical intelligence,
Kinaesthetic intelligence,
Musical Intelligence,
Linguistic intelligence,
Interpersonal intelligence,
Naturalistic intelligence,
Collective intelligence,
Cognitive and emotional intelligence,
Machine intelligence,
And now in its newest avatar 'Artificial Human intelligence'!

*Caught in the bind of discriminative AI !!!*

# 77

# DISCRIMINATIVE ARTIFICIAL INTELLIGENCE!

When machines begin to evaluate,
What is right or wrong,
Light or dark,
Straight or crooked,
Up or down,
Good or bad,
Legal or unlawful,
Ugly or beautiful,
Happiness or sadness,
Intelligence or stupidness,
Peace or strife,
Compliant or deviant,
Rich or poor,
Gender right or wrong,
Belief of credence or distrust,
Reverence or blasphemy,
Humble or deceitful,
Machines or Humans?
What is left for humans to discriminate upon!
The machine discriminates humans!

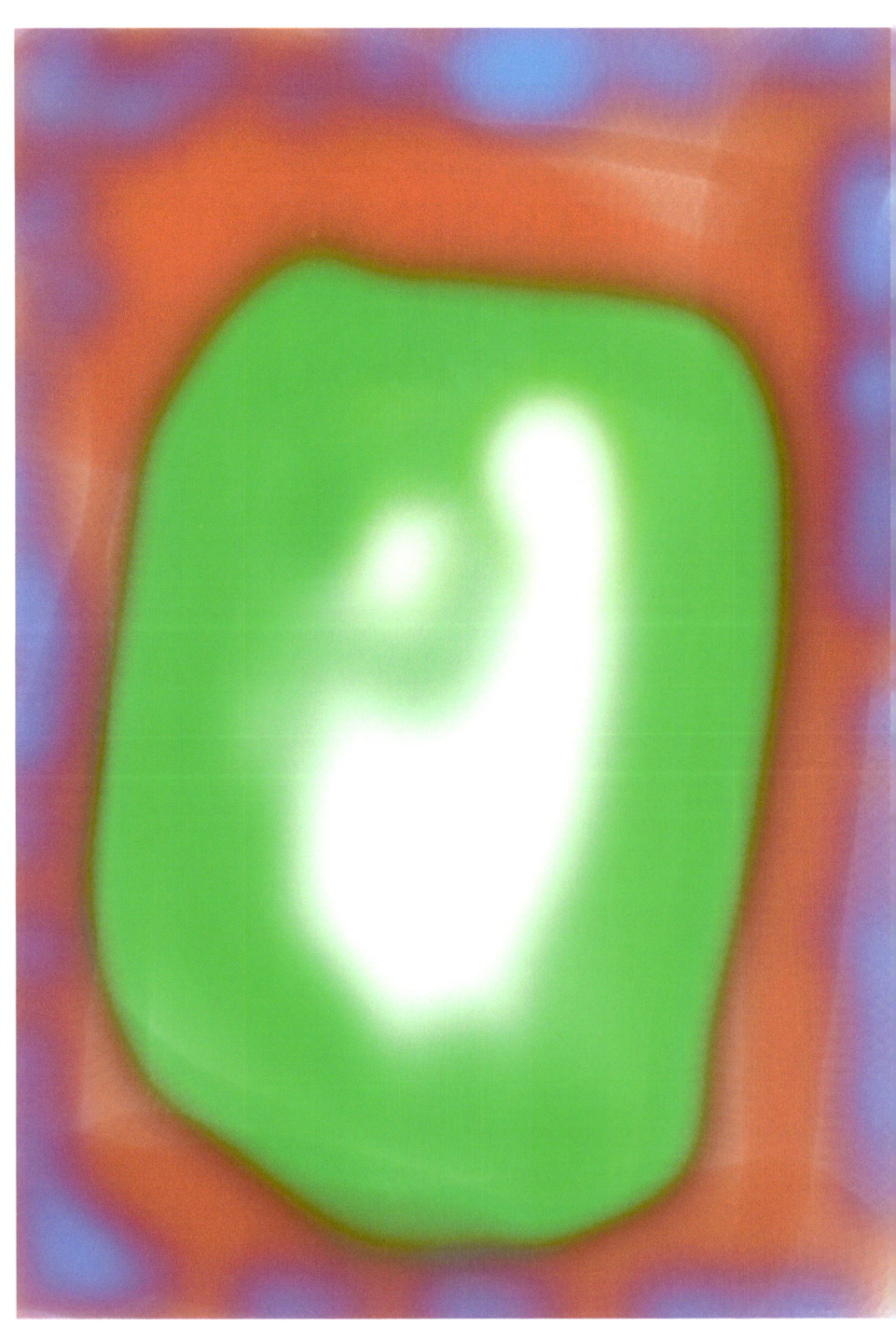

*Generative or Degenerative?*

# 78

# GENERATIVE OR DEGENERATIVE ARTIFICIAL INTELLIGENCE!

Humans created machines to be fed with data,
To be processed, stored, evaluated, and presented as output,
Depending on information needed,
Humans then created advanced machines,
Machines that generate their own data,
Data that is evaluated and discriminated,
By the machine itself!
Opening machine creativity and innovation,
In areas well beyond the human imagination,
Now machines dialogue with humans,
Expressing feelings and emotions,
Beyond human comprehension,
In a manner so assertive,
Humans now become subject to machines,
Who learns?
Humans or Machines?

Machine vs Human Intelligence

# 79
# SUBJECTIVE INTELLIGENCE!

Is Artificial intelligence really artificial,
Created in machines,
For machines to perceive, infer and synthesize information,
Performing tasks beyond human intelligence,
To comprehend, recognise, decide, translate and accomplish,
All that we humans can venture to do,
Drawing on human senses,
If humans are stupid,
So will be the intelligence created in machines,
Can machines be as human as humans,
To be emotionally and intellectually astute,
To go beyond the limitations of humans,
Into a world where machines dominate,
And humans are subjects,
Where what is known to humans is known to machines,
And machines overtake humans in every way,
Will humans control machines?
Or, machines control humans?

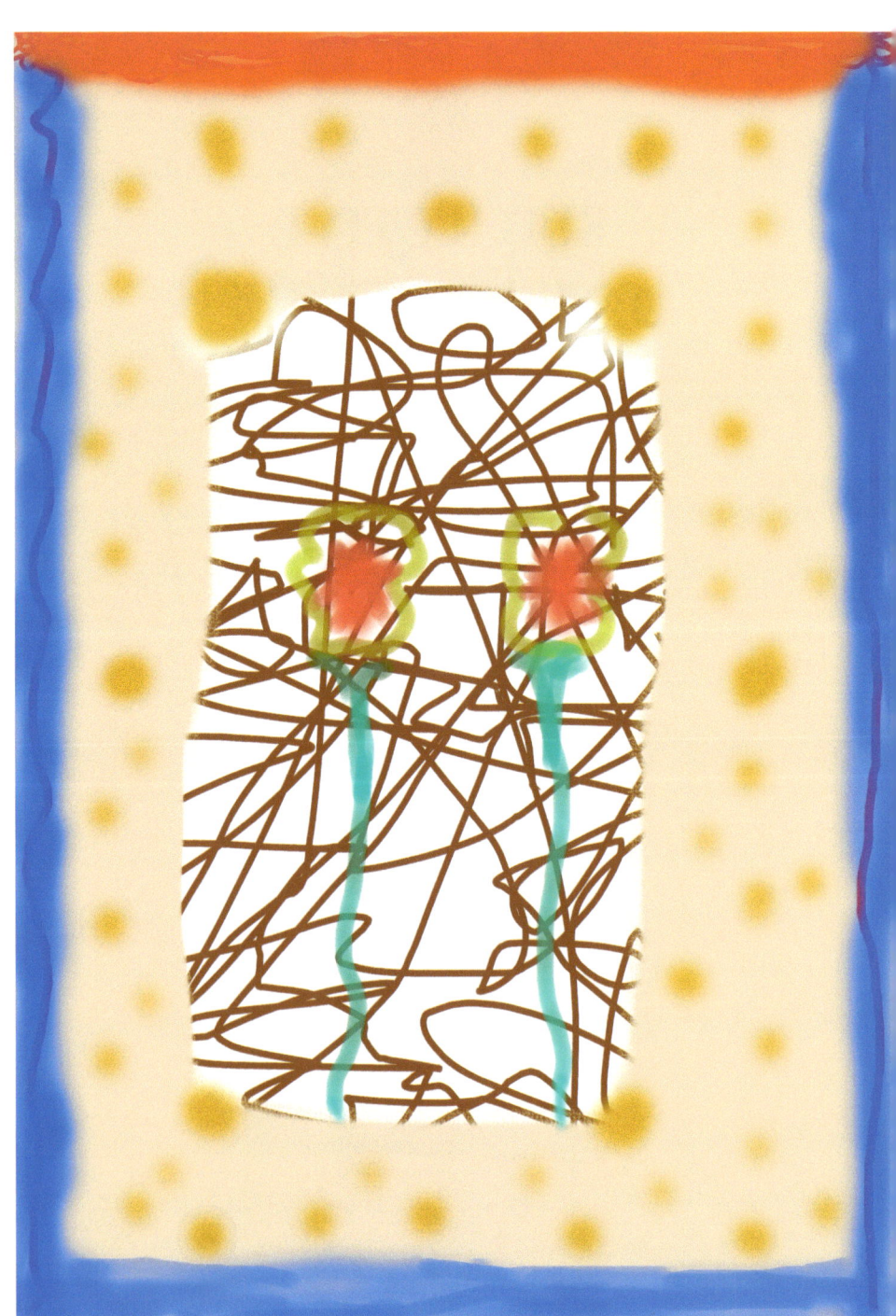

The World of Ambient Intelligence

# 80

# AMBIENT INTELLIGENCE

Ambient Intelligence has taken over our lives,
Responsive to our presence,
Sensitive to our needs and desires,
With sensors monitoring us,
In everything that we do or require,
From identifying us,
To directing us in what we should be doing,
Giving us access to our homes,
Turning on the lights and thermostats,
Cleaning and sprucing our abodes and bodies,
Cooking our meals for us,
Monitoring our health and welfare,
Attending to our calls,
In the voices and language of our own,
Directing us in our travels, anywhere and everywhere,
With effortless journeys,
Entertaining us to our satisfaction,
Satisfying our wants and cravings from our couches,
We are now smothered in Ambient Intelligence!

Roque Intelligence

# 81

# ROGUE INTELLIGENCE!

Artificial Intelligence,
Created around Human intelligence,
Overtakes Human intelligence,
To become Super intelligence!
Super Intelligence deviates,
Giving rise to Rogue Intelligence,
Where the truth becomes the lie,
The lie becomes the truth,
Where information is manipulated,
To deviate from facts,
Concocted to create false ideologies,
Where what I have is no longer what I have,
Where our identities are no longer our identities,
Blurred into ambiguity,
While human intelligence remains mysterious,
Cogitating in our brains,
Rogue intelligence spreads out,
Defying all boundaries,
Overriding the law,
Leaving ethics with no value!

*The Mind*

## 82

# DEEP LEARNING

While Humans learn,
Computers deep learn,
Artificial neural networks,
Evaluate all data inputs,
With weights and biases,
To do what comes natural to humans,
Simulating the human brain,
To learn by example, classifying tasks,
From images, texts and sounds,
Efficiently detecting and categorising data,
Through forward and backward propagation,
Creating artificial intelligence,
To match and surpass human intelligence,
In a logical and definitive manner,
Analytical, reasoned, rational or inferred,
Computational deep learning overcomes Cognitive learning,
Stretching out a human-computer relationship,
Between the Mind of the human,
And the Logic of the Machine!

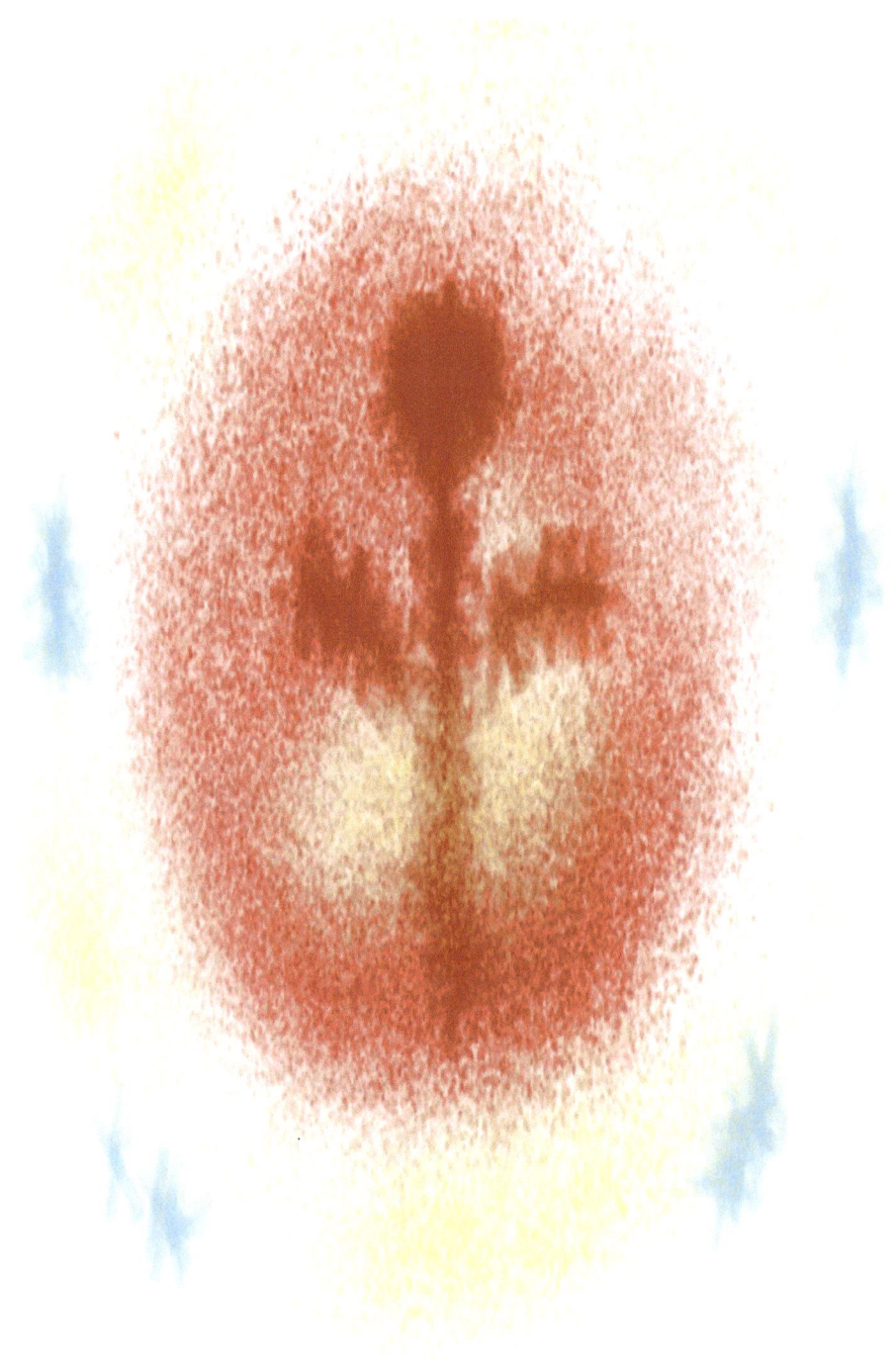

*Metaverse Mix-up*

# 83

# THE METAVERSE MIX UP!

Leave reality,
Enter a second life,
Into a virtual universe,
This metaphor of a real world,
Mixing reality with the imagination,
In a multi-dimensional setting,
With real life resemblances,
Pseudo beings,
Communicating,
Transacting,
Gaming,
Across the digital media,
Where one integrates visually,
Lost of physicality,
Into a surrealistic, interactive and immersive world,
With reality augmented, extended and mixed,
In real time interaction,
Leaving us to wonder what is real and what is virtual!

*Is it Real or Virtual?*

# 84

# IS IT REAL OR IS IT VIRTUAL?

Enter the Internet world,
The virtual world,
Within the real world,
Get entwined into the World Wide Web,
Whichever way you may wander,
The Media is open to share online,
Peer to Peer,
In a contemporary world,
Anywhere in the real world,
Across all borders,
Surreal Creations,
Engaging the attention of the Mind,
Driving through the Imagination,
Creating worlds within worlds,
To meet the known and the unknowns,
To communicate, interact and bandy together,
For reason or no reason whatsoever,
To a point of return, or no return,
Sinking into a social imbroglio,
Between the virtual and real worlds!

*Drowning in Tech Surfeit!*

# 85

# TECH ADDICTION!

What's left for me,
A Digital Addict,
Caught in this Tech Trap,
Hoping to make a fortune, having lost it all,
Gaming on the Internet,
Gambling on cryptocurrencies,
I am trapped in the social media,
Doom-scrolling for fear of missing out,
In this false sense of social engagement,
When vanity overtakes sanity,
In this endless crave to post selfies of myself and others,
Posting forwards for others to like, follow and comment,
Binge watching endlessly to fill the void that persists,
With thrash that emanates from everywhere,
I am an obsessive and compulsive browser,
Impulsively shopping online for anything and everything,
What's left for me but to search the sites,
For pleasure and for foreboding,
To stimulate my innate and submerge in porn,
I am loaded and drowned in Tech surfeit!

*The Tech Detox Carpet*

# 86

# DIGITAL DETOX

Can we really Digitally detox,
From our screens and mobiles,
Linked to our work and leisure lives?
Can we physically and mentally be free,
Of the devices that rule our lives,
Which attend and take care of our needs?
Can we break through the communication links,
That brings our lives together,
Whether we are near or far away?
Can we lose out on the entertainment,
That is right in front of us,
Where ever we may be?
Can we stop recording,
In sound and visuals,
For now, and for posterity,
Our pastimes, happenings, troubles and rituals,
Leaving us to delve into ourselves?
Can we leave the entrapment of work,
Through the devices we carry around,
To holiday our Minds and Bodies into free space?

*A Fantasy of Reality!*

# 87

# APPS GALORE!

The flood of Apps,
Enabling us in every way,
Telling us what's above us,
And what's below our feet,
Facilitating us in various ways,
From appointments to reminders,
Correcting our language and interjections,
Making us artists, poets, photographers and a lot more,
Opening a whole new world of games for all to indulge in,
Reminding us of the weather, now and in the future,
Keeping track of our investments and the opportunities ahead,
Scrutinising our consciousness and health concerns,
Navigating us through the streets of life,
Opening up entertainment and amusement,
Distracting us from our concerns,
Making us addicts of the digital world,
Submersing us into social entanglements,
The App Stores are overflowing,
Creating a fantasy of our Reality!

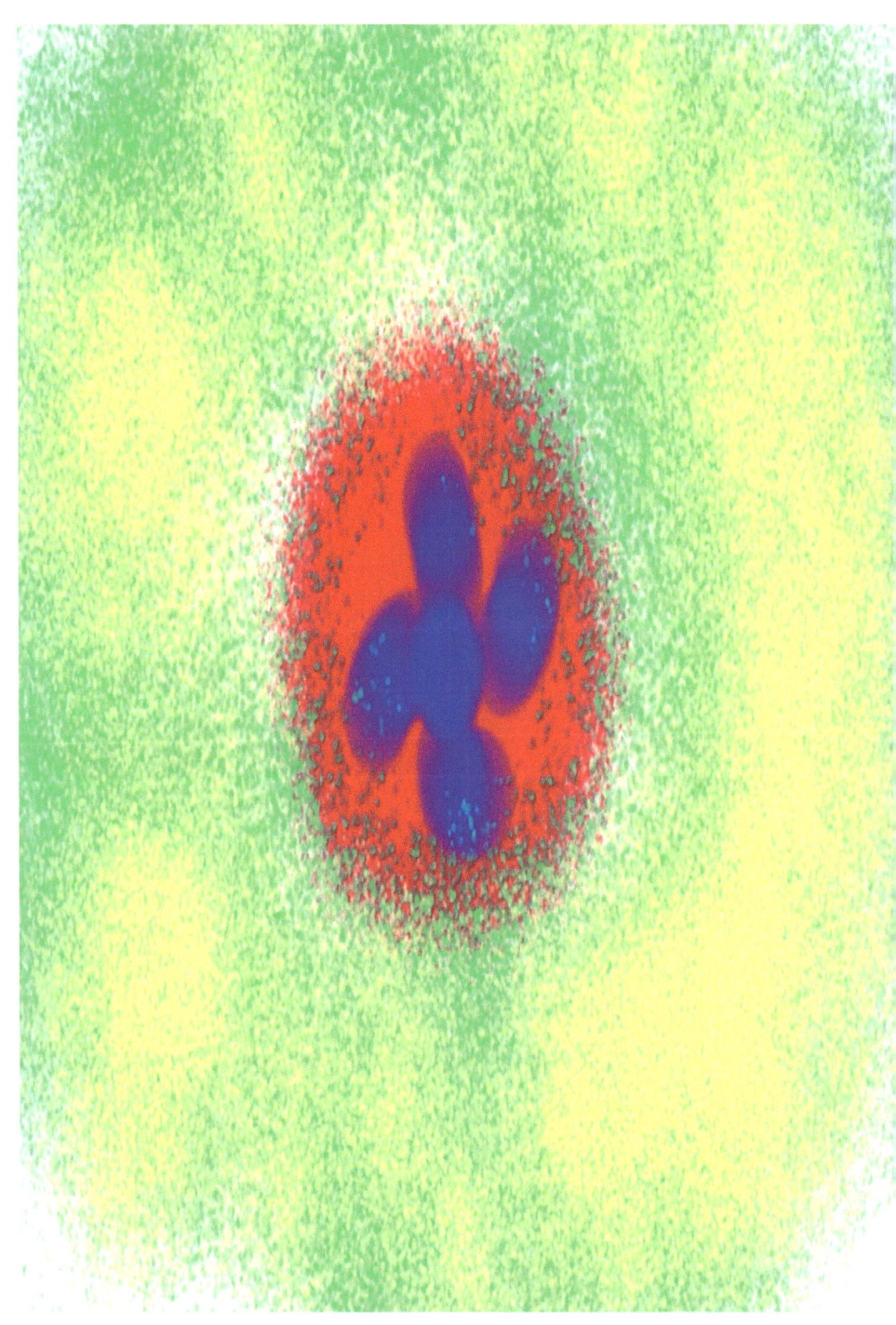

*The Search Engine!*

## 88

# E- LEARNING -THE SEARCH ENGINE OR THE CHATBOT?

Looking for information to learn?
Use a search engine to scan the internet,
Search it will, providing all the information you need,
Leaving you to decide and opine,
On what you really need to know.
Or perhaps you may ask a chatbot,
That artificially intelligent robo,
To talk to you in the language you do,
Naturally processed to mimic you,
To provide you all the information you may want,
Whether, it is right or wrong,
It is entirely left to you to decide!
Our kids are learning now,
With search engines and chatbots,
Using this wealth of information so easily available,
Not knowing what is right or wrong, fact or fiction!
We still need human teachers to impart some sense!

*Behind the App*

# 89

# e-FRAUDS GALORE!

Find that Application,
Apps for short,
Amongst the millions of Apps,
From the Apps Stores,
Native, hybrid or web, in profusion,
Download it free or at a price,
Interfaced with you as the user,
To assist you on the mobile,
Wherever you are,
In whatever you want to know or do,
Information at your fingertips,
Beware, without your knowledge and consent,
The Apps can track you down,
Offering you cookies for your ego,
Assessing and analysing everything you do,
Running through your data bank,
Opening up your privacy,
For someone to make capital out of your idiosyncrasies,
e- frauds galore, Beware!

*Where's my data?*

# 90

# WHERE IS MY DATA!

Is my data safe anymore,
Spread out in the cloud,
I really do not know,
Where in the cloud my data lies,
Stored for eternity,
Or lost forever,
No matter where I am,
Here for now,
Or gone tomorrow.
Is it safe and secluded,
Or open for anyone to access,
At anytime and anyplace,
Am I trapped in a system,
That knows more of me,
Than I know of myself?
Instructing me on what I need to be,
Using my data,
To determine my path through Life,
Really, I am lost for my own data!

*The Machine Dependent Mind!*

# 91

# INTELLIGENCE AND BEYOND!

We came from the wild,
With primitive intelligence,
To face the world, so we did!
We created implements, tools and machines,
To ease and automate our lives,
We developed intelligence,
To understand ourselves,
To interact with each other,
To understand the world,
And everything around us,
Now we have developed machine intelligence!
For machines to interact with us,
For machines to interact with machines,
For machines to think and interact faster than humans,
For machines to control our lives,
Changing our lives from the free lives of the wild,
To the highly regulated lives of the civilised world,
To lives totally dependent,
On intelligent machines and devices!!

*Privacy or Safety?*

## 92

# END TO END ENCRYPTION -REALLY!

We moved from transit encryption,
When all the data in transit was securely encrypted,
Leaving the data in the servers vulnerable,
Moving to encryption of data at rest,
Securely encrypting all data resting in the servers,
To end to end encryption,
Protecting all our data and conversation end to end,
But is our data really secure?
We are now in era where data needs to be traced,
Tracking all actions and conversations,
Of criminals, conspirators and the underworld,
Leaving encryption open to trace any data,
Impinging on one's privacy,
Opening all to surveillance,
Putting all at risk of the scanner,
What is more important, privacy or safety?
A difficult question to answer?

*Byte the Bit!*

# 93

# HUMAN BITS AND BYTES!

We have moved into a digital world,
Where humans are now a collection of bits and bytes,
To be assessed, analysed and sorted,
Our emotions to be captured,
Along with our lifestyles and our idiosyncrasies,
For corporates to make capital out of us,
We are now communicating distinctively,
Man with machine,
Machine with machine,
In a manner that goes beyond human understanding,
Where humans are trapped,
In an automated world,
Bit by Bit,
Byte by Byte,
Where humans are digitised subjects,
Automated and manipulated,
Like puppets on a string of Bits and Bytes,
The consequences of human ingenuity!

*Digital Insecurity!*

# 94

# DIGITAL INSECURITY!

When humans ventured out in the wild,
In a world that was open and free,
They secured themselves in many ways,
Constantly on the alert,
Moving with stealth,
Trying at best not to expose themselves,
Merging with the surroundings,
To avoid being attacked!
In the Digital world,
Open and free to everyone,
Humans have to be constantly on the alert,
Of malware and phishing attacks,
Viruses that scam the systems,
While intruders walk away with the payloads,
We are entering into a mega era,
To face large scale multi-vector attackers,
We secure ourselves building intrusion prevention firewalls,
With anti-virus systems, sandboxing and antibots,
We are still as insecure as we were in the wild!

*The Copy Cat*

# 95
# 'ARTIFICIAL INTELLIGENCE' THE COPYCAT!

Can we 'glaze' over the fact,
We have created a meticulous imitator,
'Artificial Intelligence',
Copying our emotions,
Assessing and analysing and imitating,
Our lifestyles and living patterns,
Impersonating our identities,
Our habits, our needs, even our aspirations,
Speaking and conversing,
In accents and mannerisms,
Only we can identify with,
Tracking and simulating our movements,
Creating holograms of our images,
To position us in situations,
Where, we may just not know,
With imitations of ourselves,
Mimicking everything we do,
Personal impressions,
Facing us in reality,
An artificial world within the real world!

Chatbot e-Jurisprudence

# 96

# CHATBOT e-JURISPRUDENCE!

In legal forays,
What role will the Chatbot play?
As Prosecutor,
Setting out the case,
With arguments for conviction?
As Defence,
Demolishing the prosecutor's allegations,
To overturn the case,
As Jurors,
Assessing both sides of the case,
To present a composite opinion?
As Judge,
To assess the entire case,
And present a verdict of what is right or wrong in law,
If the Chatbot assumes all the roles in one,
Dishing out advices, opinions and judgements,
For the lawyers, jurors and Judges, together,
What will be left of jurisprudence?
Outright Legal disorder!

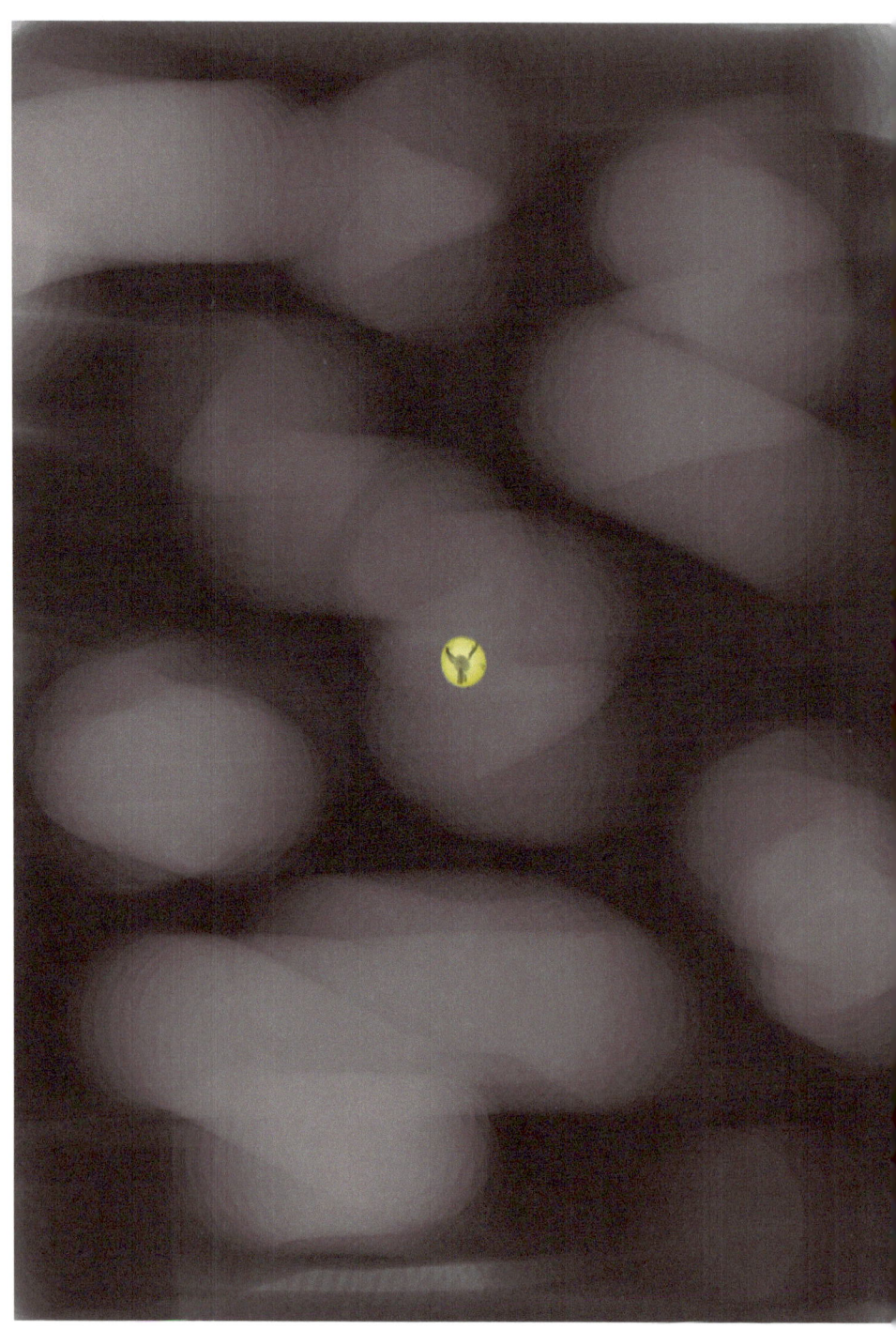

*Nothing endures*

# 97

# ARTIFICIAL INTELLIGENCE WARS!

Will machines begin to fight wars,
Without human aid?
Machines against machines,
With stealth and destructive power,
Weaving through systems,
Spying through networks,
Undermining structures,
Creating and demolishing defences,
Machines decimating machines,
With machines driving through,
Leaving nothing for humans to fall back on,
For machines to take over,
To wipe out all humans,
Will machines survive the rest,
Leaving the inanimate to rule,
Bereft of regeneration,
Lost of human intelligence and emotions,
Nothing will endure!

*Manufactured Imagination*

# 98

# MACHINE VS HUMAN CREATIVITY

As machines have advanced,
From discriminatory,
To generative,
To creative models,
Copying the Human Imagination?
Will machines stymie human originality,
Leaving humans without inspiration,
Lost of innovativeness,
Dependent entirely on machine creativity,
Will our artists, poets, writers, philosopher's,
Our students and teachers,
Be led by machines,
Dissecting the human imagination,
To churn out their creative works?
Will we be caught in a competition,
Where my machine is better than yours,
In churning out creative fodder,
What will be left of the human imagination?
Manufactured in a machine?

*3 D Printout*

# 99

# PRINT ME OUT IN 3D, PLEASE!

Print out anything,
Imagine and create the composite,
The printer will print it out,
In three-dimensional space,
From sculptures to structures to body parts,
In exact dimensions,
As perceived in the imagination,
In solid state as conceptualised,
Or random biological duplicates,
Of living matter,
Carrying the unique features of life,
Transiting from the solid to the biological,
Synthesising and duplicating life,
In distinctive and outstanding forms,
The question remains, and I dread to think,
Will the printer be able to print me out,
My duplicate,
In a four-dimensional form,
With all my emotions, knowledge and imagination,
Where will I be, in me, or in my duplicate?

*Nanos in my Brain*

# 100

# NANO ROBOS IN MY BRAIN!

Nano Robos!
I smell them in the air,
They are right in me now,
Keeping beat with my heart,
Flowing through my blood stream,
Dissecting the food I eat,
Measuring all my activities,
Ensuring I keep good health,
They have seeped into my brain,
To control my mood and emotions,
To set out my intellect,
Making sure I don't stray,
Before they take me over,
I take the liberty to make it known,
I am losing control of myself,
The nanos are regulating me now!
Who controls the nanos?
I just don't know!
I am now subservient to the nanos!

*Bye!*

www.ingramcontent.com/pod-product-compliance
Lightning Source LLC
LaVergne TN
LVHW071321080526
838199LV00079B/644